Timothy Green Beckley's
KAHUNA POWER

AUTHENTIC CHANTS, PRAYERS AND LEGENDS OF THE MYSTICAL HAWAIIANS

Global Communications

Kahuna Power

Copyright 1987
Updated and Revised 2007
All Rights Reserved c by Timothy Green Beckley
(d/b/a Inner Light/Global Communications)

No portion of this book may be reproduced in whole or in part without the express consent of the author and publisher.

World Rights are available from the Publisher who may be contacted at
Box 753, New Brunswick, NJ 08903
MRUFO8@Hotmail.com

ISBN 0938294474

Publisher – Timothy Green Beckley

Assistant to the Publisher -
Carol Ann Rodriguez

Editor in Chief -
Sean Casteel

Cover Art and Graphics -
Tim Swartz

Additional Layout -
John Anthony Miller

IT IS SAID THAT YOU CAN ATTRACT GOOD HEALTH, LOVE, SELF ESTEEM, POWER AND ENJOY THE BEST THINGS IN LIFE BY PRACTICING THE ANCIENT OCCULT ART OF "KAHUNA MAGIC"

You are about to enter a strange and unknown world made up of ancient gods who possessed supernatural powers, wandering ghosts, helpful spirits, other worldly visitors, herbal medicine men with tremendous healing powers, phantom animals, and much, more that up till now has remained strictly taboo.

The Kahuna are regarded by many as being the most psychic individuals who have ever existed on our planet, and yet so little is known about their culture.

Long before civilization came to their shores, the inhabitants of the Hawaiian Islands possessed a spiritual knowledge that placed them far beyond the realm of mere mortals.

- It is said they could bring back the dead through prayer.
- Cure almost any disease and ailment through proper use of herbs which they cultivated.
- Communicate at will with higher dimensions and the departed souls of loved ones whom they were able to contact for personal guidance and assistance in all matters of everyday life.
- Predict and sometimes control the course of future events.
- Ward off negativity, anxiety, and draw to them that which was of a higher — more positive — nature.

The powers possessed and utilized by the Kahuna are legendary and though it is today illegal for them to use their abilities, many of the descendants of the original spiritual masters of Hawaii still practice their faith in complete secrecy.

After gaining the confidence of the local Kahuna practitioners, author Timothy Green Beckley and psychic Maria Carta were permitted to enter a seldom glimpsed society and to understand a spiritual system which still offers considerable appeal to those living in today's world.

KAHUNA POWER contains the chants, the prayers and the documented legends that could improve YOUR life if you let it!

USE THE MYSTICAL CHANTS & PRAYERS OF THE SACRED HAWAIIAN HIGH PRIESTS TO POSSESS ALL YOU DESIRE & NOW!!!

KAHUNA POWER

AUTHENTIC CHANTS, PRAYERS & LEGENDS OF THE MYSTICAL HAWAIIANS

BY
TIMOTHY GREEN BECKLEY

PSYCHIC IMPRESSIONS BY
MARIA CARTA

CONTENTS

About the Authors Those Who Made The Journey .... - 7 -

Return To Paradise- Introduction To The Expanded Edition .... - 11 -

Original Introduction You Can Learn the Magical Ways of the Kahuna .... - 13 -

Chapter 1: Kahuna Magic- Can It Bring Back The Dead .... - 17 -

Chapter 2: Tapping The X-Force Of The Kahuna High Priests .... - 29 -

Chapter 3: Understanding The Hawaiian Language .... - 43 -

Chapter 4: Ghosts and Gods of Hawaii .... - 51 -

Chapter 5: Helpful Spooks, Good Spirits and Guardian Angels .... - 67 -

Chapter 6: A Dire Warning .... - 79 -

Chapter 7: Chants To Avoid Possession, Evil and Misfortune .... - 89 -

Chapter 8: Foretelling the Future and Other Occult Powers .... - 101 -

Chapter 9: Animals and the Spirit World .... - 115 -

Chapter 10: Kahuna Herbal Remedies For A Better You! .... - 121 -

Chapter 11: Ritualistic Burials- A Descent Into Hell .... - 145 -

Chapter 12: The Menehune-Leprechauns of the Pacific .... - 153 -

Chapter 13: Hawaii's Mysterious Madame Pele- Fire Goddess and Phantom Hitchhiker - 163 -

Chapter 14: Captain Nancy and the Mystical Powers of Dolphins .... - 177 -

Chapter 15: The Spiritual and Psychic Quest of Penny Melis .... - 185 -

Tim and Maria at the very start of their mystical quest for knowledge about the Kahuna of Hawaii.

About the Authors
Those Who Made The Journey

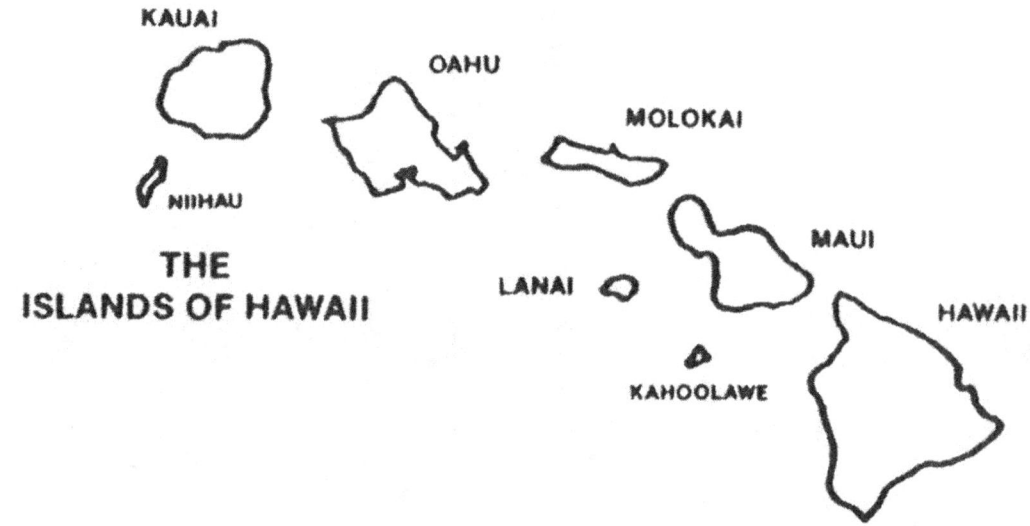

Timothy Green Beckley

The author witnesses the breathtaking sight of sunrise on the rim of the sacred Haleakala crater. It was believed the gods, including Madame Pele, resided here in the "House of the Sun" at the summit of the highest peak in North America. (photo by Maria Carta)

About the Authors
Those Who Made
The Journey

TIMOTHY GREEN BECKLEY

As a moviemaker, journalist, magazine and book publisher, Tim Beckley has covered a wide range of controversial topics in his career. He is, however, perhaps best recognized for his writings on offbeat subjects. Known in many quarters as "Mr. UFO," his articles and features on unexplainable phenomena have appeared in publications around the world. Over the past four decades, he has been a popular guest on an estimated 400 radio and television talk shows, discussing not only his personal experiences—which go back to a very early age—but has also kept the public up to date on events in this often very sensational field.

MARIA H. CARTA

Maria Carta is an especially gifted psychic whose fame is spreading rapidly. Reincarnated from Atlantis, ancient Egypt and more recently as a Hawaiian Kahuna priestess, it is only natural that she would be putting her personal touches on this particular topic. A clairvoyant since birth, Maria can chart a person's past and see into their future. She reads Tarot cards, can see the human aura, channels beings from higher dimensions, talks to spirits, can see guardian angels, and is often of help in guiding a person's life in the areas of love, finances, employment, family, friends, as well as being able to reveal karmic patterns. She is often able to give lucky numbers and bring "good luck" to those she reads for.

PENNY MELIS

As part of the research for the second edition of this book, the author was accompanied by Penny Melis, who is also a psychic with a background in the paranormal. Penny is descended from a long line of gifted ancestors, is able to sense and feel others' emotions and is tremendously in tune with the world around her. She was even able to feel her family members' pain in death when they passed on.

Return To Paradise—
Introduction To The Expanded Edition

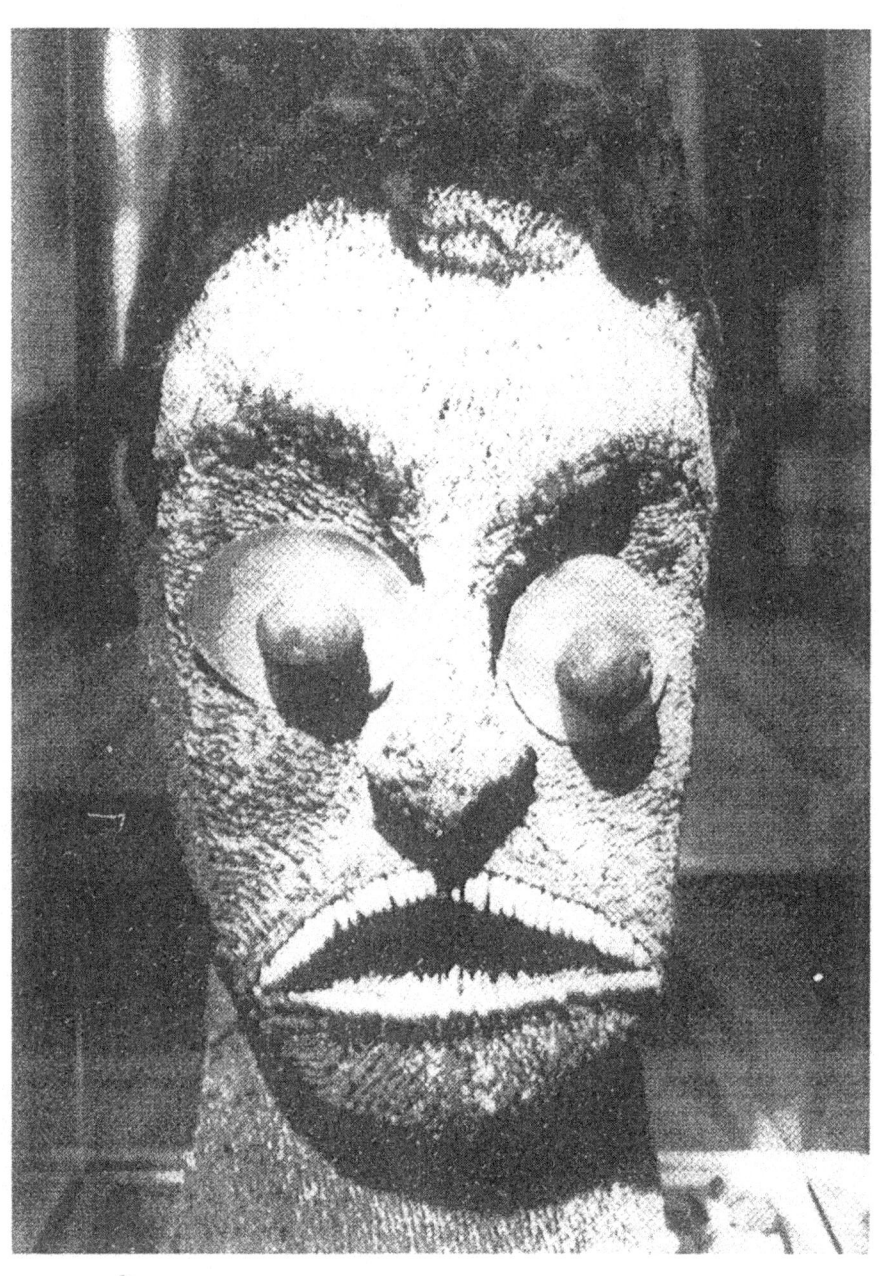

Return To Paradise – Introduction To The Expanded Edition

The weather was exceptionally good, the vibes near perfect. Hawaii on my second visit was even more delightful as recollections of my first trip to paradise were rekindled and I got further drawn in by the exotic charms of the Islands and their humble people.

The presence of the Kahuna is still evident, though it seems to be diminishing as "society" tightens its grip on the culture that is unique to the 50th state.

This time my fellow "journeymen" consisted of psychic Penny Melis, who works closely with Inner Light Publications, and her delightful daughter Mayven, a true old soul who is just beginning her journey into this lifetime. I only hope that Mayven remembers the wonderful time she had with the dolphins and our visit with the most powerful Volcano Goddess on the planet. Hopefully this edition of *Kahuna Power* will help to bring back these memories over the years to come and that she may travel back there again, as I know I shall be doing in the not-too-distant future.

There is still much more to be said about the Kahuna and the mysteries of Hawaii. I would be thrilled if readers would write me about their own mystical experiences on the Islands so that I can include them in any future commentary.

They can be sent to:

> Tim Beckley
> c/o Inner Light Publications
> Box 753, New Brunswick, NJ 08903

In addition, I would like to personally thank my friend and associate Sean Casteel for helping to reedit the version of *Kahuna Power* you are now reading, in order to bring it into perfect form, as well as a lovely new cover by veteran journalist and graphics designer Tim Swartz.

Aloha.

Original Introduction
You Can Learn the Magical Ways of the Kahuna

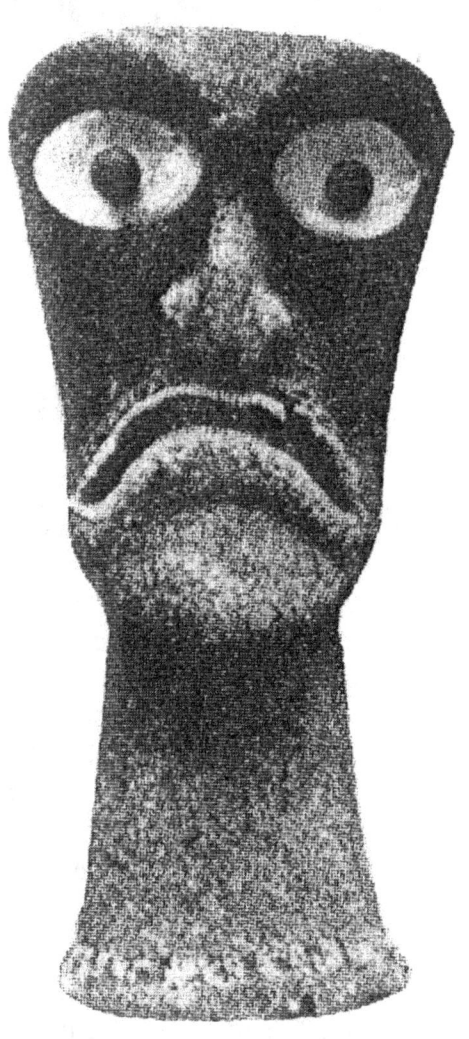

Original Introduction
You Can Learn the
Magical Ways
Of The Kahuna

As a seasoned investigator of the strange and unusual, as well as a serious student of psychic phenomena, for many years I was painfully aware of the fact that my education in at least one specific area of the paranormal was seriously inadequate. The discipline that I had not had time to probe thoroughly is known as the ancient magical art of Huna, as practiced by the Kahuna of Hawaii. In order to expand my awareness of this rapidly dying mystical and spiritual system, I thirsted to know more. What I learned can best be described as in one adjective: Incredible! I was astounded again and again by the lore that I uncovered. I was amazed by the power of the Kahuna, but was delighted to conclude that their power is within reach of us all.

The fascination began with the knowledge that the Kahuna were among the most magical people who have ever walked the face of this planet. Their understanding of human nature and herbs, plus their magical prayers and chants made them as one with the gods who were willing to do their bidding. I was enthralled with their belief that the mind has limitless powers, and that they had their own guardian angels and personal spirits who protected them and offered advice and guidance at times when they needed it most.

Are these Kahuna relegated to antiquity? Not quite! And that's the most amazing part of my research. For even though the Kahuna have died out—or given up their beliefs in favor of the more aggressive Christianity—I was able to meet and talk with a few of those who still hold true to the old customs and ways.

But more on that as we go along. The agenda I set for myself was simple. To learn all that was possible about the Kahuna high priests, I needed to talk to people who knew something about them. People like Brad Steiger, America's foremost parapsychologist. Or devoted researcher and writer, Keith Ayling, who has taken a particular interest in the Kahuna. Then there were the local experts as well, such as Kalani Hanohano, former publisher of the FULL MOON, a respected journal of island folklore and strange goings on. Pat McKinnley of Honolulu filled us in on what she knew about esoteric matters, as well as telling us about her own UFO sightings, which tie in very comfortably with the spiritual beliefs of the Kahuna, who took such things as mysterious lights in the sky very much for granted.

Finally, I felt I needed to visit the enchanted islands of Hawaii myself, not as a tourist, but as a scholar in the search for truth about these sacred rituals that might soon be totally forgotten if they are not written down for others to see and comprehend.

In order to enhance my understanding of what was involved in the lore of the Kahuna, I decided to ask a trained psychic to come along on the journey, whose job would be to pick up and interpret things I might miss with the usual five senses. I was almost certain there would be vibrations aloft "in the air" that still remained from bygone days when the gods were no doubt closer to the people who inhabit the picturesque string of islands in the Pacific.

Such a practice was not without precedent. For example, noted scholar and author, Dr. Jeffrey Goodman (*We Are The Earthquake Generation*), has for several years been experimenting with what he termed "psychic archeology" in which a person, adept at receiving clairvoyant impressions, will visit the site of historic ruins and, while in an altered state of consciousness, be able to actually see and hear events as they took place centuries ago. I also understand that the Russians have trained several of their best psychics in this regard, hoping to utilize their services to locate lost continents, including the mystical island of Atlantis. So, as unusual as my undertaking might seem, I was not operating totally on untried ground.

After much consideration, I selected Maria H. Carta of Staten Island, New York, to make the six thousand-plus mile trip with me. An exceptional psychic with an acknowledged gift of ESP and clairvoyance, I knew she would be useful for the purposes stated. Her job would be to take mental notes on our expedition, which I could later incorporate into parts of the completed manuscript. Throughout this book, you will find Maria's psychic impressions italicized. I feel her help was invaluable, and that others hoping to accomplish what I set out to do will consider using such individuals in their work. For truly with Kahuna, we are dealing with a lot more than "meets the eye"; we are dealing with invisible realms, with other dimensions, and with incredible forces which continue to baffle those less objective than I.

But after all has been said and done, I feel subsequent to my in-the-field research among the beautiful Hawaiian people, that I came away with the knowledge that anyone can, just like the Kahuna, tap into this "high source" of spiritual power. And that anyone can draw near to the "infinite source" that guides us all.

I hope that you, the reader, will learn much from this book, that you will be entertained and enlightened enough that you will want to go on your own "vision quest," not necessarily just to Hawaii, but to other parts of the world where there is a long heritage of mysticism and magic to make us intrigued.

--Timothy Green Beckley
New Brunswick, New Jersey

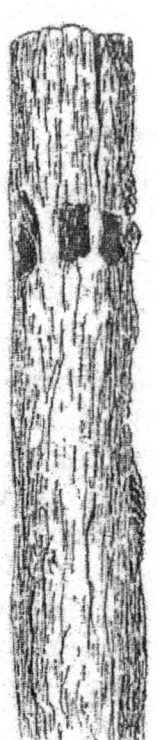

Chapter 1:
Kahuna Magic— Can It Bring Back The Dead

Timothy Green Beckley

Kahuna Magic – Can It Bring Back The Dead?

The minute Tim and I arrived in Hawaii, I could feel the change in my vibrations and energy. As I closed my eyes and absorbed the sunshine, I psychically imagined the islands as they existed a little over a century ago. For although Hawaii is still exotic in many respects, civilization has closed in and taken away at least some of the natural beauty of this paradise.

Like most tourists, before leaving the mainland I had read up on the islands and their history, and even tried to get ahold of some very hard to come by literature on the Kahuna. What has been written on the subject is, for the most part, very "Westernized," and gives little of the true picture of the religious and mystical practices of the original Hawaiians who nearly all vanished from sight.

My clairvoyant gifts—and the fact that I lived on the islands in a previous life—revealed that the Kahuna were among the most powerful mystics spiritual leaders the world has ever known. Nobody alive today—not even someone as famous as Uri Geller—can perform the incredible feats of magic the Kahuna did as a matter of course. The high priests, for example, were adept at all forms of holistic medicine (apparently possessing a cure for cancer). Much like the Egyptians, they were pioneers in many fields, including science, music and mathematics. I feel strongly that the early Kahuna priests did, in fact, hail from Egypt. It seems they practiced various forms of white and black magic and were into ceremonial magic, just as the high priests in Egypt did. They displayed the ability to use mind over matter in moving objects and in controlling people at a distance. They were very religious and worshipped the elements, which had the strongest impact on their lives. They could control the weather, look into the future, read the minds of humans and animals, and travel through space utilizing a form of out-of-body projection. Like the American Indian, the Kahuna were great warriors and often invoked the Vital Force to win at battle. The Kahuna were, it seems, at the center of the entire Hawaiian culture.

--Maria H. Carta

◀ ▼ ▶

WHO ARE THE KAHUNA?

The mere mention of the word "Kahuna" strikes fear in the hearts and minds of many otherwise rational people. Why? Mainly because the Kahuna were thought to be witch doctors who could literally will a person to die even if they were many miles away.

And while it is true that some Kahuna practiced a type of "black magic," the word Kahuna has, in reality, a very sacred and spiritual meaning.

"Kahuna" simply means "keeper of the secret," or "heart lore."

A Kahuna was a priest, a minister, a sorcerer, or an expert in a profession. He might have been a doctor, surgeon, scientist, herbalist, navigator or musician. The secrets of the Kahuna's trade were carefully guarded so that they did not fall into the wrong hands. A high priest would only pass on his knowledge shortly before death, usually by whispering into the ear of his successor who he had personally chosen to carry on his work.

Nobody knows for sure how many Hawaiians still follow the "old religion." Most of what was known has either died out totally or has gone underground because of the religious fanaticism of the Christian missionaries who tried their best to erase all that had gone before and replace it with their brand of God and religion.

As Maria and I were to find out, however, the Kahuna have not all passed away. A handful (again, nobody really knows how many) still continue on with the work of their ancestors, practicing powerful ceremonial magic when the moon and the tide is "just right," just as their fathers and grandfathers before taught them the ways of the ancient gods.

KINDS OF KAHUNA

There are various types of Kahuna. The dreaded one is the "Kahuna 'ana 'ana," who was the power to pray a person to death.

The medical Kahuna is skilled in combining religion and psychology. He has a knowledge of diet, herbs and health. He knows, for instance, that the aloe plant is the perfect balm for burns. The "awa" is an extract of a shrub that is used as a narcotic drink. The medical Kahuna uses it as a sedative when he must set broken bones. The extract also figured in ceremonies conducted by the Kahuna to exorcise evil spirits and to placate the gods. Scientists today are probing into an anti-cancer serum concocted from a certain sea worm—a possible cancer cure used by the Kahuna for centuries.

There is the Kahuna Aloba, a love-inducing specialist. The Kahuna Pule is a priest or prayer specialist. The Kahuna Ho'opi'o can inflict illness by rubbing his own head to give a severe headache to another. The Kahuna Lomilomi is an expert in the art of massage. The Kahuna Ho'ohanau is an obstetrician. He has the power to grant a pregnant woman a painless delivery. He does it by taking the pain upon himself or by transferring it to the father.

Fortunately, the power of the Kahuna has not died in Hawaii. In 1974, the new penal code enacted by the state no longer condemns the Kahuna as it had done for many years. The Kahuna is now permitted to bless new roads, buildings, bridges, hotels and even homes.

The new law, however, has a negative side. Anyone can claim to be a Kahuna even if he has *not* been trained and does not know the Hawaiian language. The true Kahuna knows how to deal with these false prophets. A simple chant usually scares them away.

A'ole oe, not keis halau
You are not of my school

No laila a'ole no oe
Therefore you cannot know

I ike I ko'u po'opo'oe
The depths of my understanding

This chant, I might add, is an excellent one to do if you feel someone is trying to unjustly take your job away from you. In fact, the remainder of this book is full of Kahuna prayers and chants that can work for you in a variety of ways. We only ask that you use this knowledge for kindness and good, and not for negative and selfish purposes.

MAX FREEDOM LONG

My association with the late Keith Ayling has given me much insight into the history of the ancient Hawaiians. Before his death, we talked several times on the subject. I never tired of listening to Keith, for he had made a study of the ancient magic of Huna and had written extensively about his findings. Yet, always willing to credit others, Keith surprised me one evening by saying, "The real authority on the Kahuna is Max Freedom Long, a scientist and archeologist. He's devoted a lifetime of study to it."

I prodded him into telling me more about Long.

"Well," he says, "this strange religion of Huna existed in ancient Egypt about 2600 B.C.E., at the time of the building of the Great Pyramid, and possibly as far back as 50,000 B.C.E., in Atlantis.

"According to Max Long," he continued, "the Kahuna were the actual builders of the pyramids because of their superhuman powers. They had control over what is known as the *Vital Force*. With it, they were able to negate gravity and transport huge stones and set them into place.

"This *Vital Force* was extremely powerful. The Kahuna received it by direct invocation to the Supreme Being. You know, there are many authorities who believe that the huge stone-moving feat was not exclusive to Egypt. They point to the existence of massive stones in other parts of the world—like Britain's Stonehenge, the monoliths of the Galapagos Islands and the giant statues of Easter Island."

"What you're telling me," I interjected, "is that the Kahuna were everywhere."

"Very nearly," Keith replied.

Keith explained that when he was in India, he spoke with a Hindu holy man who said that the priests of MU, a lost continent that predates Atlantis by many thousands of years, knew how to invoke the *Vital Force* and thereby nullify gravity and change the vibrations of matter in such a way that it could defy the other forces of nature, including heat and solidity. The Hindu mystic also stated that when Christ walked on water, he demonstrated the power of the *Vital Force*. Known, too, to the ancients were magnetic healing, spirit materialization, bodily transportation and levitation.

KILLING A MAN USING THE VITAL FORCE

Keith said, "The Hindu then gave me a demonstration of the *Vital Force*. He selected a stick at random on the ground and held it over his head. He chanted an incantation, and after a few minutes he placed the end of the stick on my forehead. I felt something like an electrical shock. It didn't hurt, but the charge seemed to flow through my entire body."

The Hindu priest told Keith: "That is just to show you that the *Vital Force* of the ancients still exists. If I wished, I could render you dead and restore you to vitality at will. One day you people in the West will discover and use this divine power just as you discovered and used electricity, although you do not know exactly what it is. But you are not ready for it—not yet."

I asked Keith, "Will we ever be ready for it?"

The crossed poles at the entranceway and the huge upright images directly behind, warn that this is highly sacred ground. The "Taboo" area contains both the Temple of Ahu'Ena Heiau (a place of peace and prosperity where help from the gods for the king and his people were invoked through rituals and the sacrifice of food—no humans or animals), as well as the Mortuary of Kamehamena where his bones were once kept (photo by Tim Beckley).

He shrugged. "All I know is that the ancient Kahuna did use the *Vital Force* as a defense against physical violence, and they employed the same method the Hindu used on me. They used powerfully charged sticks, which they tossed at the enemy. On contact, the enemy forces were rendered senseless.

"You can also find in our own American history books that some Indian medicine men allegedly had the power to render a man unconscious simply by touching him with a supercharged finger."

Keith Ayling told me about Dr. William Brigham, who, until his death, was curator of the Bishop Museum in Honolulu, which I later visited myself. Brigham conducted lengthy and painstaking research into the activities of the Kahuna priests on the Hawaiian Islands, and stated that the Kahuna had actually raised men from the dead. They did it by pouring this *Vital Force* into the corpse while ordering the human self to return to the body.

BRINGING BACK THE DEAD

"Authorities on the Islands," said Keith, "have testified to being eyewitnesses to these miracles. In one case, an American doctor was present when he saw a Kahuna restore life to a boy who had been pronounced dead 16 hours earlier.

"Brigham came to the conclusion that the Kahuna miracles were based on a form of consciousness in which the priests were able to perform the so-called impossible acts through concentrated prayer. While in this form of consciousness, they used a force which allowed them to control temperature, affect the density of matter and perform healing."

Keith was asked to explain what happened to the Kahuna after the Great Pyramid was built.

"I can't," he said. "No one knows why they disappeared from Egypt. Dr. Brigham and Max Freedom Long spent nearly 70 years in research on the subject. They traced some members to the Pacific and some to the Atlas Mountains in North Africa. The latter became known as the Berber Kahuna."

Keith told me that the sole survivor of the Kahuna of ancient Egypt was found in Africa, a Huna priestess. It was she who provided a vital clue in the form of Huna words which stemmed from the same source as those used in Hawaiian dialects. Deciphering these words was no easy task, since the Hawaiians had no written language until 1820, when the first missionaries arrived.

"Without a written record," said Keith, "it's almost impossible to trace the routes the Kahuna took after leaving Egypt. They may have gone to ancient

Greece, Latin America, Rome, India, China, the Philippines and to the aboriginal tribes of Australia. But we do have some solid information concerning their migration to North Africa."

THE HIGH PRIESTESS OF ATLAS MOUNTAIN

Keith told me about Robert Stewart, an English writer who was dedicated to the study of ancient religions. Stewart had spent his youth with a Berber tribe in a remote spot in the Atlas Mountains. He was 13 when an aged woman gave him and her 12-year-old daughter daily talks on the history of the tribe. She told Stewart about the Huna conception of God on each level of consciousness, with emphasis on the High Self, which means the soul or the super-conscious mind.

Stewart reported that the priestess demonstrated the power of the High Self by bringing him and her daughter to the top of a mountain. She ordered birds to come and listen to her message, which they did. Flocks of them perched on rocks. The procedure was also done with snakes: deadly rattlesnakes, puff adders and other reptiles crawled to the woman and stayed quietly until she ordered them to leave.

Keith said: "This highly unusual woman told Stewart that man's High Self was capable of interlocking with the god and thus avail itself of the *Vital Force*.

"She demonstrated the power of the High Self by telling Stewart and her daughter to hold a piece of stone in their hands and say a prayer. Without using any force at all, the stones in the children's hands turned to dust."

Stewart reported that his studies were interrupted in 1938 when the woman was struck and killed by a stray bullet during a tribal war.

THE STRANGE STORY OF ANDREW CROSSE

Keith Ayling was the teller of many unique tales, but the most incredible of all was the case of Andrew Crosse. It had a twist at the end that gave me chills, when I first heard it, and it still affects me virtually the same way today.

Keith said: "Crosse appeared in Somerset, England, at the turn of the century. He inherited an old estate and used it to make experiments in a makeshift laboratory. He had little knowledge of science, yet one day he announced that he had discovered the secret of life.

"It happened one day while he was trying to develop an artificial crystal by charging an ordinary stone with electricity. When he failed, he tossed the stone into a dish—and was then amazed to see the stone disintegrate into dust. But it was not the kind of dust we're used to seeing. It took on definite shapes and the shapes appeared to be insects. Two days later, the insects sprouted legs and tails. They crawled out of the dust and moved about freely. However, within a week they were all dead.

"Crosse hurriedly wrote a paper to a learned society in London. Scientists flocked to his house to watch a second experiment. They saw the rock crumble to dust and saw insects form. Yet because they could not explain the phenomenon, they branded Crosse as a fraud. One of the scientists tried the experiment himself, but failed.

"Crosse was heartbroken. He knew he was not a fraud, yet he had no way to prove it. Rumors spread through his neighborhood. People said he was a witch. He was tormented in the street. He was not able to show his face any longer. Then one night there was a blinding flash that came from his laboratory and his house went up in flames. By the time the fire was put out, there was nothing left of Andrew Crosse except his ashes.

"The man had no relatives and few friends. Little was known about him. But several years after the fire a female medium held a séance on the site of the fire. She stated that Crosse was the reincarnation of a Druid priest. The Druids were said to have used Huna magic when they erected those massive pillars at Stonehenge."

DID THE KAHUNA BUILD THE GREAT PYRAMID?

The cosmic forces used by the Kahuna were not restricted to one place. Keith Ayling noted that the Berber woman mentioned earlier told Stewart that her ancestors had built the Great Pyramid in Egypt. And they did it by asking their Higher Selves to cut the huge stones and carry them to where they were needed.

The same kinds of pyramids can be seen in Mexico and Peru.

"Apparently," said Keith, "their builders were familiar with what we call apports, which is the phenomenon of moving great objects over long distances by what is known as mental control. The theory is that the object is thinned out before it is moved, then its density is restored after it has reached its new location."

He cited a study of the Holy Men of India, in particular one Sai Baba, who is able to produce food and precious stones out of the air and to transport himself form place to place at will.

"Some authorities believe that the Kahuna's knowledge of apport may have been responsible for the 500 huge stone statues on Easter Island. Some weigh 50 tons and are mounted on platforms 15 feet high."

Whenever the few inhabitants of Easter Island are asked about those sneering stone faces, the stock answer is: "The Great Magician moved them with word of mouth." The feeling is that since the original settlers on that island were Polynesians, it's quite possible that among them were Kahuan priests who had knowledge of this apport.

"Actually," Keith continued, "there is evidence that this is so. In 1932, on Easter Island, tablets bearing ancient writings were excavated. They resembled similar Kahuna artifacts found in Hawaii.

"Also, Thor Heyerdahl of Kon-Tiki fame revealed that he came across legends in Mexico and Peru which were identical with those of Easter Island. What he said was that the Incas, the Mayas, the Polynesians, and the inhabitants of Easter Island all had the same name for the Supreme Being."

THE GOD LONO AND CAPTAIN COOK

According to Hawaiian legend, Lono was the god of rain, fertility, harvest and prosperity. After a quarrel with his wife, he left home and wandered aimlessly. He did, however, promise to return. It was believed by the Hawaiians that Lono would appear at Kealakekua Bay, which was sacred to him.

Every year, the natives held a makahiki festival in honor of Lono. Oddly enough, it was at this exact time of year that Captain James Cook sailed into the cove in search of refreshment. The date was January 17, 1779.

Cook's ships, the Resolution and the Discovery, were greeted by 10,000 Hawaiians who paddled in canoes, swam in the bay or stood at the shore—all convinced that the god Lono had finally returned.

Cook noted in his log: "I have nowhere in this sea seen such a number of people assembled in one place." There were some 3,000 canoes afloat in the bay. On shore, white kapa banners were held aloft on crossbars. These were the ancient symbol of Lono, and they looked very much like Cook's mast and sails.

Captain Cook was further astounded when he went ashore. The natives bowed low and covered their faces until he passed. And during the next two weeks, the British sea captain was the guest of honor for sacred ceremonies. He was inundated with fine gifts. Boxing and wrestling matches were held for his pleasure. He was called Lono, for surely he was the ancient god who had finally returned to this sacred cove.

But the party ended rather abruptly and Captain Cook fell out of favor. It happened on February 4, when the two ships sailed out of Kealakekua Bay. A fierce winter storm smashed the Resolution's foremost, forcing Cook to return to the bay for repairs.

Few natives were there to greet him now. The festival was over and the Hawaiian chief, Kalaniopuu, had placed a kapu (taboo) on the area. There were some natives around, but they were rather cool to the visitors. They began to doubt that Cook was Lono because a god would not suffer such damage.

The natives began stealing from Cook's stores, little things at first, and then more and more, until the items stolen represented quite an enormous loss. Finally, on February 13, the Discovery's cutter was cut loose and stolen.

Captain Cook was enraged. He ordered the bay blockaded, then went ashore with nine men to take Chief Kalaniopuu hostage until the cutter was returned. That did not happen. The Hawaiians were waiting for them with clubs, rocks and daggers. The British had rifles, but they were no match against the swarming warriors. Five of the crewman escaped; four did not, and one of them was Captain Cook.

Later, a delegation of Hawaiians returned parts of Cook's body. Most of it had been burned. A bundle of the captain's bones were wrapped in fine kapa barkcloth and a cloak made of black and white feathers. Inside were Cook's hands, recognized because of a scar, the scalp, skull, lower jaw, thighbones and an arm bone. The rest of the body had been dispersed among the chiefs.

In retaliation, British crewmen bombarded the villages, set fire to temples and killed scores of natives. Two of the frightened Hawaiians were decapitated, their heads stuck on poles and displayed on a rowboat. The two ships then sailed away. It was February 22, 1779.

Missionaries later stated that Captain Cook had committed blasphemy by permitting the natives to venerate him as a god.

Chapter 2: Tapping The X-Force Of The Kahuna High Priests

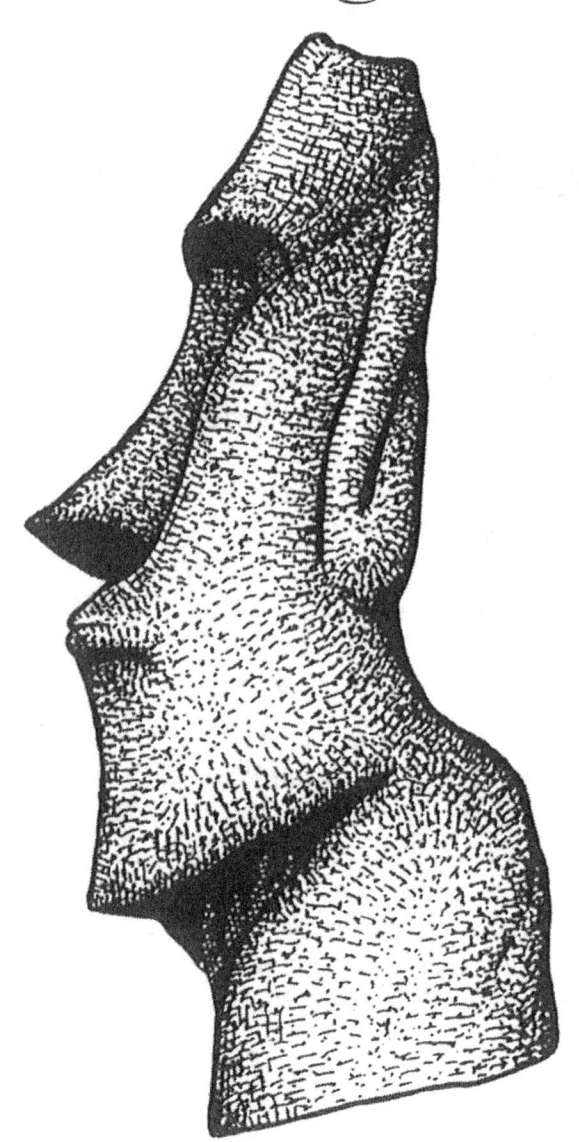

Tapping The X-Force Of The Kahuna High Priests

*My experience as a practicing psychic tells me that there are forces in nature which we cannot see, feel or smell, but once we have learned how to correctly control these forces—or the **mana** of the universe as the Kahuna identified them—we grow in power. The priests of Hawaii were masters at tapping into what has been called the **X-Force**. Today, parapsychologists speak in terms of the human aura and invisible life forces which have been photographed through a process discovered in the Soviet Union. Known as Kirlian photography, scientists working in various university laboratories have discovered a mysterious energy surrounding every living thing. The Kahuna knew about this force centuries ago, and applied their knowledge either for the betterment of their community or, if angered, to harm their enemies.*

The Kahuna worked by themselves, but also in clusters because they realized that the collective energies produced by a group can be considerably stronger than those manifested from a single individual operating occult magic alone. The Kahuna were metaphysicians, or perhaps they should be termed the first New Agers. They knew about diet, about breathing, about exercise and believed strongly in the powers of the mind to control everything that existed in the world around them. They also practiced the laying on of hands and knew that it was important to cleanse the chakras of the body in order to open them up to higher learning.

--Maria H. Carta

Visitors to the Islands must not be afraid to ask questions if they wish to learn about the "old system." Fearful of reprisals by those unfamiliar with their beliefs, most Hawaiians dare not talk about what they learned as a child from their grandparents. Sure, they may know quite a few of the old prayers and chants, but what would be the advantage of sharing them with non-believers?

THE PRAYER OF A KAHUNA KUNI

Ia Awaiku ka us I Lanikeha
The spirits of Awaiku send rain from the heavens of Lanikeha

Ka ua maawe au e Kane
The fine rain of you, O Kane

E Kane pakanaka
Kane who touches humanity

Kane pamakana
Who warns us by his presence

Mahana kaua ia oe, e Kane
You and I warm to each other, Kane

The above prayer is only one of many that I heard during my visit to Hawaii. I talked to numerous Hawaiians and learned that a goodly number of them still believe in the ancient religion that has its origins in the dim mist of time. I learned that the Kahuna, powerful sorcerer priests, still manage to maintain their grip on that religion.

From obviously sincere individuals, I heard frightening accounts of ghost dogs with eyes as bright as fire that prowl the night, of ghosts of people, of giant armies called the Kamehameha's warriors, of mysterious deaths brought about by black magic and certain prayers. I heard accounts of miraculous cures and of the little people who do things you can't do yourself.

What I did more than anything else while I was in Hawaii was listen. I listened to young people and old people, to priests, to anyone who would tell me about this great culture.

Timothy Green Beckley

SECRET CODE OF THE KAHUNA

The wise men of ancient Hawaii were devilishly shrewd. They were the ones who created the language, but because they were also Kahuna they wanted to be sure that they could talk to each other in the presence of commoners without being fully understood. They accomplished it by inserting into the root meaning of words several definitions that were sometimes not even remotely connected with each other. This was especially true in the secret code of the Kahuna priesthood (Ke oihana kahuna) with their double, triple and even quadruple meanings. Those admitted into the secret circle were able to converse freely, while others were misled. A Kahuna would know the secret meaning of a word by the way the speaker pronounced it and by noting the context in which it was used. The ali'l (chiefs) used words that only they knew; the people of the common class listened, but could not comprehend.

HUNA MAGIC

I have the great fortune to know one of the greatest authorities of all on the mystery of the Kahuna. His name is Brad Steiger. Nearly twenty years ago, Steiger developed a close association with Max Freedom Long, the grand old man of Huna magic. Long's research on the subject began at the turn of the century. When Steiger came along, Long shared his books, tapes, notes and clippings with him. It was a windfall for Steiger, and of course for me, because Steiger has been generous enough to share his knowledge with me.

Steiger said: "For centuries, the Kahuna practiced a system of magic that was so powerful that it enabled them to control the winds and the weather, to foresee the future and sometimes to change the future. They had the ability to heal the sick instantly, to walk over hot lava and hot coals, to read minds, to send and receive telepathic thoughts—and sometimes, it is said, even pray their enemies to death.

"The system of the Huna was the power system of the Polynesian Islands at the advent of the white man and his religion. Western culture could not compete with the Kahuna priest on his own terms, so it instigated a program of limiting his practice, legally, through the political structure. In a little more than a generation, the native Americans in Polynesia had overwhelmingly embraced Western culture, along with its style of dress and its religion. There are only a few practicing Kahun on the Islands today."

Brad Steiger, author of **American Indian Magic** and the **Star People** series, told me that most of the Kahuna have gone underground. You can find a few who will do some grandstanding rituals for the crowd, just as voodoo worshippers might do for tourists.

When Stieger went to Hawaii for the first time in February 1972, he met Reverend Eddie Kung, a Kahuna who was the son of a Kahuna who had great healing powers. Steiger also met a Kahuna named Morna Simeona, who told a tale of Kahuna magic in which a great bulldozer was interfered with in a mysterious way because it was trying to rip up sacred burial grounds. State officials were furious in their attempts to confront the power of the Kahuna priests.

Of course, the Kahuna are still underground because the legislature outlawed black magic and sorcery some years ago. But if you talk to certain natives, as I did, they will tell you, almost in a whisper, that the practice continues. The law has not prosecuted anyone for practicing Kahuna magic, but it does have teeth in it, and, if invoked, can be brutal.

It's not unusual in Hawaii to see a Kahuna standing along with a Catholic priest or Protestant minister during groundbreaking ceremonies or dedications.

Not long ago, on the Island of Maui, workers started to excavate a hillside overlooking the ocean to build the Sheraton Maui Hotel. Somebody noted that the workers were digging up an old cemetery. The builders knew better than to fight the magic. They put on a big luau in which six pigs were roasted and consumed. And while that was going on, the Kahuna chanted away evil spirits that might have lurked about.

Also on Maui, a family moved into a new house and in no time one of the family members became sick. It was discovered that the home had been erected over a burial plot. A Kahuna was called in. The priest prayed away the troublesome ghosts that haunted the place. The patient recovered.

What I've learned by talking with Brad Steiger and others is that trying to find out how the Kahuna get their magical powers is an impossible task. The secret has been guarded for centuries (some say the fifth century), and no one outside the clan will ever find out what it is.

Probably the most famous Kahuna of all was David K. Bray. Hawaiians held him in great esteem. He was duly honored in a resolution approved by the Territorial Legislation of Hawaii shortly before Hawaii became the 50th State of the Union. The resolution acknowledged that Bray had been a practicing Kahuna for more than 50 years, and it commended him for his "great contribution to the people of Hawaii." He was a High Priest of the Sons and Daughters of Hawaiian Warriors, the oldest Hawaiian society, and was regarded as a master and leading exponent of old Hawaiian chants. He was also in demand for ceremonial blessings.

Apparently afraid of nothing, the author attempts to tap the X-Force of the Kahuna who once practiced their powerful magic here, while images of the various spirits guard this place which was a refuge for the priests (Photo by Maria Carta)

THE POWER OF GOOD AND EVIL

Kahuna-ism is potentially the most dangerous occult science anyone can toy with. It can be used for great good, but also for horrible evil. It all depends on the orientation of the deeds and thoughts of the practitioner. The Kahuna were essentially spiritual and used their powers for practicing "white magic" to help and uplift mankind. The priests who practiced white magic obtained their mana from the divinities to whom they prayed for knowledge and aid. They were taught from a very early age how to meditate, to concentrate with the undisturbed power of positive thought, and to cause things to happen through the powers of faith and worship.

But there are also the other kind of Kahuna, the kind who practice "black magic" for evil. They cast spells on people and make them do horrendous things. Recently, in the Fiji Islands, an eight-year-old boy was found decapitated. Police later arrested an 18-year-old youth and charged him with murder. The killer confessed that a witch had put a spell on him, promising him immortality and seven dollars in cash if he would bring a child's head. The unofficial conclusion was that a Kahuna had hexed someone. A couple of years ago, on the Island of Maui, a businessman died suddenly. An autopsy showed that he had been the victim of a heart attack. But was he? An investigation turned up the fact that the businessman had enraged a Hawaiian family over a business deal, and that they had asked a Kahuna to pray him to death.

I heard an intriguing story while I was having a bite to eat in an out of the way place on Maui. A neighborhood man told me that when he went to school, he and his friends organized the first Junior Police Officer unit on Maui. One boy was something of a wise guy. He was forever going into places that were off limits to the students. The man said that he told the smart aleck that if he didn't stop doing it he would take him to the principal.

That was not a smart thing to say, as the brash boy was someone special, and that if anyone did anything to him, he would be crippled. The warning was ignored and the fresh kid was reported to the principal.

My friend said: "Sometime later, I was walking along the street with my father when my foot suddenly swelled up. There was no break in the skin, and I had not turned on it. My father rushed me to a clinic, but the doctor was unable to do anything for me.

"I was really scared. I told my father about the fresh kid, so he immediately went to the boy's parents. They knew my father, but what they did not know was that I was his son. They promised him that they would undo their work.

"The swelling in my foot went down almost immediately. I was cured. Was it sorcery? Black magic? I don't know. I don't even know if the fresh kid's parents were Kahuna, but they worked some kind of magic on me, that's for sure."

Interestingly enough, some authorities say the Hawaiian Kahuna never practiced black magic until the Christians came to the Islands. At that time, the Polynesians adopted some of the Christian rituals and worked them into their own, and were able to call upon demons for help. Other experts disagree, saying that Hawaiian sorcery goes back in time and perhaps even to India, where the Polynesians might have originated.

The only real fact here is that no one knows how the sorcery started because there are no written records. In any event, the Islanders believe that there are supernormal powers, that they are really part of nature, and that the Kahuna are able to command the spirits of the dead to work miracles for both good and evil.

Fortunately, the majority of the Kahuna practice their mystic arts for the good of people. The Kahuna lapa'au is a doctor who can affect cures by psychosomatic methods as well as physical means. He also used herbs in his cures, and some of these cures appear to be miracles even in the eyes of skilled surgeons. Some practice divination by reading the formation of clouds. They are the Kahuna kilokilo. The Kahuna Nana'uli are weather prophets.

ANOTHER KIND OF MAGIC

In the Gilbert Islands there are Kahuna who have the power to talk to porpoises. The playful swimmers are called and respond immediately, even swimming over reefs to reach the Kahuna. In Tonga there are those who are able to talk sweetly to sharks so that they swim to the side of the boat. The sharks are then roped and caught.

It does seem odd that these primitive people can do what our super-intelligent scientists can't do, that is to learn the language of the porpoise. It makes us wonder whose magic is stronger.

THREE SOULS

Brad Steiger explained to me that the Kahuna sees each person as having three souls or spirits that reside inside. They are called the *Unihipili*, the *Uhane* and the *Aumakua*. The *Unihipili* is like the subconscious. The *Uhane* and the *Unihipili* work as a team. Each needs the physical medium of the human body. The *Aumakua* is composed of a male and female essence. It has a balance and polarity that is necessary for working any magical system on the earth plane. The *Aumakua* is called the High Self and is actually the highest god the Kahuna deal with. They had always known that there was a Supreme Being, but never assumed that they could pray to it.

Brad explained to me what the Aka substance is. He said that the Kahuna belief is that there are three invisible bodies surrounding the three souls. They are the astral doubles of these spirits. The Aka can also be likened to ectoplasm. The Aka substance is sticky, which explains how one can touch an object and symbolically connect himself to the Aka thread of the person who owns the object. The spirit self then travels the Aka thread to the other person to gain information about him.

MANA

Mana is a vital force that resides in every human body. The low self uses the force called *Mana*. The middle self uses a force called *Mana-mana*. The high self uses *Mana-loa*.

Mana can be likened to body waves, which have been recorded in laboratories. Mana-mana is really brain waves. Mana-loa is like the Holy Spirit, the force that moves through all living things and can create miracles.

THE HIGH SELF

Steiger says that in his studies with Max Freedom Long he learned that when a Kahuna wants to perform magic he must call upon his High Self. This is where all the power is. To reach the High Self, the Kahuna contacts the Low Self, which is connected to the High Self by the Aka cord. When contact is desired, Mana must flow up the Aka cord until the High Self is reached.

According to the Kahuna, the Low Self is the seat of memory. It is the storage area for the Middle Self's thoughts. In the Kahuna discipline, thoughts are things. They exist. They have dimension. A thought is a tiny bead of Aka substance, which clusters about other tiny beads of thought.

The Middle Self contacts the Low Self to make the connection with the High Self, when the Kahuna so desires it. However, with the young who are studying the discipline, it is not always possible to make the connection. A blockage appears. Often, an external spirit is to blame. And just as often it might be a negative emotion, like pride, fear or guilt. The Low Self might have done something for which it is ashamed, and does not want contact with the High Self.

After hearing all this from America's number one author of psychic books, I was aware of the fact that the Polynesian Kahuna were far ahead of the so-called civilized world in their thinking processes.

THE X-FORCE

An intangible energy known variously as the *X-Force*, the *Vital Force* or the *Unknown Energy* is reached by the Kahuna by correctly using the Ha Prayer Rite. To perform any kind of magic, one must contact the High Self, wherein lies the intangible energy.

If you follow the ritual step by step, and with enough practice, you can accomplish the feats of telepathy, clairvoyance and miracle healing that the Kahuna do today in secret.

The elements of consistency and repetition must be emphasized here. They are important. The High Self must receive a clear picture of your desire or situation. It cannot be muddied up with contradictions or a constantly changing image. The correct image must be fed constantly to the High Self. You should be careful in choosing the prayer you wish to make. Know ahead of time the image you are going to send to the High Self. If you think clearly with a definite image in front of you, you won't have to worry about offering the High Self a confused request.

The first step is to take four deep breaths. This should be done very slowly and in much the same way a yogi does his breathing exercises. What you are really doing is allowing the Middle Self to instruct the Lower Self to create more Mana. Once this Mana or Vital Force is aroused, it is held in waiting for you.

The extra Mana in step two waits for the subconscious to reach along the shadowy Aka cord until the High Self has been contacted.

The third step comes in when the Low Self releases the Mana in a kind of sacrificial gift to the High Self, which will use its force to formulate the answers to your prayer.

The fourth and last step sees the mental image you've created rising up the Aka cord with the Mana to the High Self.

There is no fifth step, but we might call repetition the fifth step. We need to get the Mana up to the High Self because without Mana the High Self is weak and is unable to accomplish anything.

You can also accumulate an excessive amount of Mana in your lower self by standing in the star position: feet wide apart and your arms extended at the sides, shoulder level. Then say again and again: *The universal light force is flowing through me now. I feel it!* For added insurance, take four deep breaths.

The secret shared by a Kahuna friend is this: "Whatever you desire, believe that you have it, and you shall have it." My source also told me that you must have faith that your High Self is taking care of the request. There is no time limit. Some requests take longer than others. If there is a spirit intervention, there will be trouble. The High Self may never receive the request. Also, if you have a sense of guilt in your subconscious, your prayers may be stifled.

The most important part of the Ha Prayer is that you cannot use it for emotional or physical harm to another.

The High Self is utterly trustworthy. It will not engage in any action that is destructive. The same can't be said of the Lower and Middle Self; if they do some harm to someone, they do so on their own, without any help from the High Self.

HOW A KAHUNA MAKES TELEPATHY WORK

One Kahuna I spoke with gave me a lot his secrets, one of them being how he communicates with a person some distance away and how he reads minds. The Aka is important here. That shadowy body material must have a thread cast out so that it can connect itself to the person you want to communicate with.

The Kahuna visualizes this connection. He does this in detail, imagines the Aka thread piercing the body and attaching itself to the Aka of the other person. Now that contact has been made, low mana of the Vital Force can flow along the thread. That done, your subject's thoughts are presented to the focus of consciousness of your Middle Self. In effect, your subject's thoughts are your thoughts. If it is done correctly, you can read a mind or communicate with someone far away from you.

YOU CAN CHANGE YOUR FUTURE

The Kahuna believe that great events of the future are already set and can be foreseen. An individual's future, however, because of his short life span, can be seen only months or years ahead. In the Huna system, the future of an individual can be changed.

The High Self constructs the future out of the thoughts and imagination of the Middle Self. Sleep is most often the time when thought forms travel up the Aka cord to the High Self. The reason for this is simple. Consciousness barriers are lowered during sleep. Sleep consciousness is more suggestible and therefore more easily reached.

If you are really interested in changing your future, the best time to actively influence the thought forms chosen by the High Self to be used in forming the new future is in the sleep state.

The subconscious is capable only of the most rudimentary powers of reasoning and is extremely impressionable. If you can lodge a thought in it, there would be no trouble with the subconscious handing that thought to the High Self.

Inputting thought forms into the Low Self can be done quite easily during sleep by using a tape recorder to play the message you want. At first you may wake up when the recorded message turns on, but after awhile you will adjust to the disturbance and sleep through it.

YOU CAN PRACTICE MIRACLE HEALING

It must be said at the outset that what a Kahuna does to perform the miracle of healing is not for you to use as a substitute for seeing a doctor. Practical medical treatment must come first. You must remember that the Kahuna priest did not achieve his greatness in a few short months or years. He will tell you that he studied for his priesthood from the time he was old enough to know right from wrong. We can tell you what he does to achieve a miracle of healing, but we don't advocate that you follow suit.

The instant healing involves three factors: 1. A High Self with a superior form of mentality and an ability to do the work. 2. The Vital Force of Mana, used in all miraculous works. 3. The flesh, bone and blood of the injured limb, and the Aka, or shadowy substance of the patient.

The Kahuna say this shadow body or Low Self is a mold of every cell of the body. It also assumes the general shape of the body.

To heal a broken bone, the High Self dissolves the injured bone and injured tissues into ectoplasm. The shadowy body mold is made of a substance (invisible) that cannot be injured or broken. Using the mold of the normal limb, the dissolved parts are re-solidified in that mold, and the result is instant healing.

The Kahuna still practice instant healing, even if they must do it primarily in secret. Nor does anyone today forget the great Lilia, the Kahuna la'au kahea, who in 1921 caused an American's arm to heal overnight. It had been infected for nearly a year and was about to be amputated by a surgeon who had given up trying to save it. The story made all the papers and cannot be disputed.

Another Kahuna astonished me with some facts about the great strides in medicine the Kahuna healers had made long before European doctors were even aware of the value of such basics as sterilization and anesthesia.

He told me that in Hawaii, medical men had dealt successfully with such ailments as ulcers, heart trouble, epilepsy and cancer. The Kahuna lapa'au (doctor) examined the patient and either treated him or sent him to a specialist. If the problem was fairly simple, the Kahuna prescribed medicine for a number of days, ordered rest, restricted the patient's diet and then ordered the kind of purge which would cleanse the body of wastes.

Internal ailments were treated with herb mixtures and sea animals. Occasionally, a few inorganic substances were used. Surgery was frowned upon. However, the Kahuna were able to remove eye cataracts by using the razor sharp edge of a certain kind of grass.

The priest told me that minor surgery was done when necessary, such as circumcision, lancing and abortion. The Kahuna doctors were able—and this is truly amazing—to replace parts of the skull with pieces of cocoanut shells and bone sections taken from other skulls.

Then there was Awa, which Hawaiian doctors gave their patients to drink as a tranquilizer. The soporific worked on the spinal cord. It was also used to curb the appetite of an obese person.

Awa is a root, and it was used to treat enuresis and insomnia. The koale (morning glory root) acted as a counter-irritant for sprains, broken bones and dislocations. It was also applied to arthritis and rheumatism sufferers because it gave off a soothing heat. Pia (arrow root starch) was administered for internal bleeding and diarrhea. Anyone in shock was given salt water immediately. Salt water was an antiseptic for open wounds and taken by the aged as a mild laxative. A natural water soluble iron oxide called Alaea was prescribed for someone who lost a lot of blood, to women with excessive menses, and to patients who complained of being tired all the time or who had lost their appetite. Turtle oil (bonu binu) used over a period of time removed scars that were not pitted and erased unwanted lines from the face. Kahuna doctors recognized that there were certain antibiotics in the earth because their treatment for a puncture wound was to make a poultice of soil and apply it directly to the wound. (More on herbs and their benefits are to be found in Chapter Nine.)

Medical men in old Hawaii knew the dangers of communicable diseases. The seriously ill patient was placed in isolation in a small house built for that purpose. After the person recovered, the house was destroyed.

I learned from an informant that the ancient Kahuna medical men were quite adept at diagnosing illnesses. They did it by smelling the sick bed, the breath, or the excretions. They watched the kinds of insects that were attracted to the urine and spittle of a patient. The specialists in those days were much like the specialists we have today. There were the following categories:

Kahuna la'au lapa'au ------ *pharmacologist and general practitioner*

Kahuna lomilomi ----------- *physio-therapist (masseur)*

Kahuna haha ---------------- *diagnostician*

Kahuna koholua ------------- *surgeon (minor surgery)*

Kahuna ha'iiwii ------------- *bone specialist*

Kahuna ho'ohanau --------- *obstetrician*

Some of the old Hawaiian medicines are being examined today by scientists looking for a cure for cancer. They are extracting an anti-cancer serum from the tentacles of certain sea worms. The serum has been tested on laboratory animals so far, but the results are reported to be quite good in arresting certain types of carcinoma.

Chapter 3:
Understanding The Hawaiian Language

Understanding The Hawaiian Language

Though this book can't justifiably be classified as a scholarly text, to understand the magic of the Kahuna and to appreciate the Hawaiian culture, it is necessary to at least know a little something of the beautiful language by which the kindly people of the Islands once communicated.

Indeed, the language of the Hawaiian people is magic in itself. To hear them speak is that rare encounter that can rightfully be classified as a mystical experience.

For one thing, the Kahuna believed strongly in the power of the spoken word, much more so than they did in the written word, and that is why they never kept a record of anything. They believed that specific words could make you well, while uttering other words might have the power to kill. Those who believe that the original colonizers of the Islands might have journeyed from Egypt have some strong backing in that the Egyptians also believed very strongly in this type of magic. The Kahuna also believe that if two people shared the same name, it was only natural for them to share the same personality traits. Since I am a practicing numerologist and astrologer, I know that there is a certain degree of truth to this statement because the vowels and consonants of certain names correspond to specific numbers, which, when added up, total the same amount.

The Hawaiians also used numerology and astrology while creating their alphabet. It is interesting to note that Pythagora (the father of the number) based his original concept on the principle of seven, and there are seven consonants in the Hawaiian alphabet.

--Maria H. Carta

Sometimes, in later years, it is necessary to be reeducated in our thinking. The Hawaiian language is similar to no other language, and so it takes some getting used to. When you master the tongue, you realize it was well worth the effort.

Captain James Cook managed to collect a short vocabulary of Hawaiian words, which he entered in his log. There were 250 words recorded. Until a New England missionary party arrived on the Islands in 1820, no one had ever attempted to write the whole language. The Americans formed a committee to study the spoken words and decided that the Hawaiians had twelve letters in their alphabet. There was a profusion of vowels in their speech, with seven consonants. It was a difficult task because the speech did not easily render itself into English letters, so much of it was lost in the process of becoming a written language. Nevertheless, two years after the missionaries landed, Elisha Loomis printed an Hawaiian-English speller. It was the area's first locally produced book.

The Hawaiian language belongs to the Malayo-Polynesian language family. It has a rich musical quality and has been described as a language suitable for poetic emotions, for singing, chanting and praying.

THE ALPHABET

All of the vowels in the Hawaiian language are pronounced as they are in Italian. All Hawaiian words end in a vowel, while there may be a complex vowel combination in the word itself.

The consonants are h, k, l, m, n, p and w. Some Hawaiians feel that there is an eighth consonant, which looks in English like an apostrophe ' and in Hawaiian is called the 'okina. The symbol represents a glottal stop. This same kind of stop can be found in several English dialects. You can find it as a stop-and-start-again kind of pronunciation. Example: A Cockney might talk of having a little bottle of beer. It might come out as a li'l bo'l a beer. In our own American Southwest, the word button might be heard as bu'n, or cotton as co'n.

In Hawaiian the consonant w is sometimes pronounced as a v sound. When the word begins with a w, the letter is often pronounced as a w: Waikiki or Wahiawa. When the w is found somewhere in the middle of the word, it might be pronounced as a v: Hale'iwa and Hawi.

Hawaiians have two types of vowels—short and long duration. A bar marks the long duration vowels, and in Hawaiian it's called kahako, and in English it is macron.

	SHORT DURATION		LONG DURATION
A as in cat	mana (power)	A as in father	nana (look)
E as in bet	hele (go)	E as in hay	nene (native bird)
I as in beet	pili (grass)	I as in beet	wiwi (skinny)
O as in boat	holo (run)	O as in boat	lolo (paralyzed)
U as in boot	hulu (feather)	U as in boot	pupu (hors d'oeuvre)

WORD POWER

One of the Kahuna who spoke to me stressed the fact that there is great power in words. He did not indicate that this was the secret of his mystical abilities. I felt at the time, and still do, that the secret of the Kahuna will never be revealed, and that the few remaining high priests will die off with their lips sealed.

But the Kahuna told me that there is a strength in words that far exceeds mere communication. Our modern science has made the same discovery, and it is something that is discovered again and again throughout the ages. High-tech experts tell us that their computers have revealed that people with the same names often share the same personality traits.

The Kahuna have also learned that the power of words can be at its greatest during the careful composition and rendering of prayers. My learned priest told me that in training one learns the prayers and rituals handed down from the past. The words are never changed. When a prayer was found to accomplish what it was set out to do, the prayer words remained the same, and will continue to remain thus through eternity.

Words were the only link between the Kahuna and the aumakua, or spiritual attendant. By remaining in constant touch with the all-seeing force from the other world, by using the proper words at all times, the Kahuna were able to cause things to be done.

Stone artifacts such as this one exist throughout the Pacific. They were left by the Hawaiians and others as a tribute to their gods. This fellow now rests on the grounds of the Bishop Museum. (photo by Tim Beckley)

"DESIRE" – THE MOST IMPORTANT WORD

According to my Kahuna friend, he who invokes must have desire. It is a powerful word, strong enough to remove all obstacles. He said desire must be kept high while fixing the mind on the objective. If the objective is something material, there is little problem; if the objective is in the abstract, one must select something material with a name similar to the objective.

TEST YOUR KAHUNA POWER

The Kahuna gave me this test, which I now pass on to you. There is nothing mysterious about it, but it does work!

Select something material that you would like to have. Make it something that is beyond your reach, but not ridiculously so. What you are trying to do is build confidence in yourself. Picking something that is so far beyond you that it is impossible to achieve would only destroy that confidence.

Print the name of the object you desire on a card. Place the card in a position in which you are able to see it often. Every time you see the card, visualize it in your imagination. Every time you do that your desire for it will become very strong. Repeat this every day. Eventually your desire will become a reality.

The Kahuna parted with this so-called secret only because it is something which has been taught over and over again through the ages.

GLOSSARY OF OFTEN USED HAWAIIAN WORDS

I was grateful to Walter Smith's book, **Legends of Wailua**, for the glossary below. Smith was born on Kauai, and was a member of a well-known Kamaaina (child of the land) family. He was intensely interested in all things concerning Hawaiian legend and spent much time researching the facts and legends of old Hawaii.

The Smith family started the Wailua River motor boat operation in 1946 and are responsible to a great degree for its development into one of Hawaii's major attractions for visitors.

Ae	Yes	Luna	Overseer
Ai	Eat	Mahope	Bye and bye
Aikane	Friend	Maikai	Good
Alii	Chiefs, nobles	Mahalo	Thank you
Aloha	Hello, farewell, love	Malihini	Newcomer
Hale	House	Mak-e	Dead
Hana	A bay, in place, work	Manu	Bird
Haole	Foreigner, white person	Nani	Beautiful
Hele mai	Come	Niu	Cocoanut
Hiamoe	Sleep, asleep	Nui	Big
Huhu	Angry	Ono	Sweet
Hula	A dance	Pali	Cliff
Ilio	Dog	Panini	Cactus
Kahuna	Priest, sorcerer	Pau	Finished
Kala	Money	Pilikia	Trouble
Ka-ma-aina	Old timer	Pohaku	Stone
Kane	Man	Pua	Flower
Kapu	Forbidden, sacred	Pupule	Insane
Kaukau	Food, eat	Puu	Hill
Keiku	Child	Ua	Rain
Kokua	Help	Wahine	Female
Lani	Heaven	Wai	Water

Tragically, we must report that the Hawaiian language is dying. About 2,000 people on the Islands still speak it, but the young are shifting the emphasis to a Pidgin English that is a corruption of both Hawaiian and English. The expectation is that in another generation Hawaiian will not be spoken at all.

Hula dancer bedecked with *lei*, or garlands.

Chapter 4:
Ghosts and Gods of Hawaii

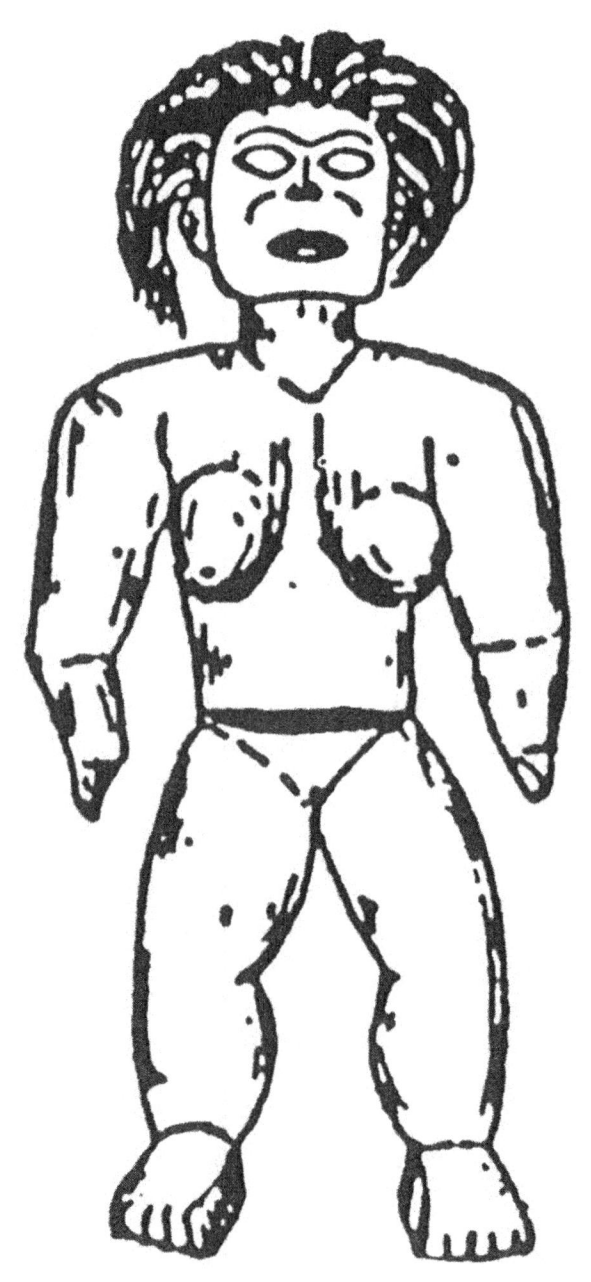

GHOSTS AND GODS OF HAWAII

One almost gets the impression that there are more gods and spirits floating around in the Hawaiian etheric regions than there are people living in this wonderful land. The truth is that there are so many living gods that nobody can recount them all. Therefore, there is even a name for all the gods as a group.

Hawaii is also rich in ghost stories. Everywhere you go, it seems someone has had a spooky experience to recount. Of course, it's easy to dismiss such otherworldly epics as just so much tall tale telling. However, anyone who is versed in the supernatural can tell right off if a story has "substance," or if it is just so much will-of-the-wisp.

Much of the information we extracted from our travels and conversations shows that ghosts and spirits in Hawaii are not much different from the ghosts and spirits to be found in other parts of the world. Only the names are different. For example, the **Lapu** fits the general description of a poltergeist, and it has been brought to our attention that these ghosts like to tease and torment their victims by sometimes sitting or lying on the victim's chest, thereby making them short of breath. On our trip, we spoke with researcher Kalani Hanohano, who says the ghosts have been seen in several of the modern hotels in Honolulu because these fancy establishments have been built on top of ancient burial sites, causing the spirits to become restless. I feel very strongly that there are a multitude of ghosts to deal with on the Islands, not only due to the fact that Hawaiians were buried on sacred grounds, but due to the number of those on both sides who were killed in Pearl Harbor and throughout this area during World War II.

--Maria H. Carta

◀ ▼ ▶

It was our first night on the island of Kauai on the last leg of our tour and, to say the least, we were disappointed about having to return to our respective homes in just a few days. After downing a typical Hawaiian dinner—a literal feast—we had decided to go for a walk along the beach to unwind after a hectic day of air travel and packing and unpacking our bags for the tenth time.

We were sitting on a partially decomposed tree stump looking out at sea when suddenly a flickering light caught my attention. Out of the corner of my eye, to my left, I saw some movements along the water's edge. There seemed to be several sources for the light, as if a small group of people were walking toward us with candles in their hands.

Now normally, I'm not easily frightened, but there was something really eerie about these flickers that made my stomach feel queasy. Within moments, I pointed out the bobbing and weaving orbs of light to Maria, and together we tried to peer through the pitch-blackness to see if we could see beyond the lights and perhaps pick up some human forms. We couldn't!

"Something's not right here," I remarked to Maria, and together we decided to leave our lonely spot along the shore of the ocean.

On the way back to our hotel, we wondered if we hadn't wandered upon some moonlight lovers on the beach, or perhaps—being a bit more sinister—someone signaling to drug smugglers on a boat a short distance offshore.

ARMY OF THE DEAD

It wasn't until the next day that we were to hear about the reputed existence of the so-called *night marchers*, or the *army of the dead*, as they are sometimes called. Anyone who you speak with about them will tell you the same thing: their advice is, when you see them, run in the opposite direction as fast as you can! The Kahuna tell us that they can be seen on dark nights when only the stars illuminate. It was on such a night that Maria and I encountered the unidentified flickers of light along the beach. From what we discovered, it was lucky we decided not to around too much longer.

Chris Cook is a reporter for **The Garden Islander**. His assignment was to interview Maria and I for a front-page story in the paper. Having been born and raised in Woodbridge, New Jersey, the youthful journalist was anxious to know what was going on back home. It just so happens we grew up only a few miles apart and therefore had a lot in common.

After concluding the interview and taking a few photos, it was my turn to ask the questions. I was eager to hear what Chris had to say regarding the legends and lore of the big island. Did he believe in the local "superstitions"? Had he ever encountered anything unusual since moving permanently to Hawaii?

"Well, yes, now that you mention it, I did have at least one experience that might interest you." Chris began his paranormal saga by mentioning that he was working near the Coast Guard Station across from Maui. "During time off from my job, I was fooling around on a sacrificial altar that has been on the beach for God knows how many years since the Kahuna utilized it in some ritual. I put my head in the slot where the priests decapitated their victims and even stumbled across a couple of old bones which were sticking up partially out of the ground."

Chris went on to say he had "set up camp near this altar, when one night I awoke to the sounds of hundreds of people walking around me. I couldn't see anything in the darkness, but the noise of the footsteps marching in unison was getting louder and louder, until I decided I should split as it didn't appear to be safe where I was camping out."

Though Chris won't say for certain, he feels there is a good possibility that the sounds might have been made by the notorious *army of the dead*.

"I had heard the various legends which say that if you see the ghost marchers, you have to join their progression for all eternity or at least until somebody takes you place in line," Chris said.

It's hard to say, but just *maybe* if Maria and I had stayed a minute or two longer on the beach, we might now be part of a ghostly progression of spirits that are doomed to walk the Islands until the end of time.

The reporter wasn't my only source for such eerie material on the night marchers. A woman told me that she and her husband were walking late one night in a remote part of Ka'u. There was no moon, but lots of stars. It was quiet, except for the lowing of cattle in the distance. The woman was frightened by the sound, but her husband assured her that the cows and calves had been separated that morning and were now calling out to each other.

But this was not ordinary lowing, the woman told me. There were voices and soft laughter. "In the distance, with the blackness of the a'a lava as a background, we saw lights moving. They were coming at us. My husband suddenly grabbed my hand and pulled me away. Together we ran as fast as our legs could go until we reached the ranch house. We had witnessed the dreaded night marchers."

I asked her what would have happened if they had not run. She replied that their fate would have been disaster or death.

Apparently, the night marchers are the spirits who displeased the gods and were not permitted to Po (Heaven) upon death. The same can be said for the lapu. The Hawaiians tell me that if one leads a good life and harms no one, he will enter Po. The bad ones in life obviously continue with their evil ways after death.

THE UNIHIPILI SPIRIT

We should also mention the Unihipili ritual in which the bones of the dead are kept in the house rather buried at sea or in a volcano. When an ancient Hawaiian could not part with the bones, he or she called upon the Unihipili spirit for help.

"Death corrupted the flesh and blood," the Kahuna explained. "It did nothing to the bones. His immortality lay with them. The Unihipili ritual kept the spirit in the bones and it was the method of deifying them.

"When a man died, his flesh was removed and dropped into the sea," the wise one continued. "This was done only by family members and they had to go through a purifying ritual after the job was done. By keeping a dead man's bones, the survivor announced that he or she was reluctant to let the deceased go to the spirit world. Often, the skull was kept in a calabash and hung from the rafters in a Hawaiian home. It was also common for a loved one to clean the leg bones, arm bones and skull of a lover, husband or wife, wrap them carefully in clean material and take them to bed. The feeling was that this helped to keep the spirit alive.

"When a person decided to bury the bones, he had to be sure to find a secret place because an enemy might desecrate the bones and thereby desecrate the spirit. Royal bones were allegedly buried in the cliffs above Kaaawa on the north shore of Oahu. No one has as yet found the caves. Iao is the famous burial cave of Maui. The last chief to be buried there was in 1736, but no one has been able to find the entrance."

At Waiuli on Maui there is a deep pit where the bones of common people were thrown. Also on Maui is a disposal pit called Kaaawa inside the crater of Haleakala. Pa'ao, the famous Kahuna, is in the burial cave of Pu'uwepa in Kohala, Hawaii. The entrance here is said to be under the sea.

Another burial pit is located in the pali of Molilele in Ha'u, Hawaii.

If a family was related to the fire goddess Pele, bodies of the dead were hidden away until the flesh decomposed. The bones were then carefully cleaned and taken to the Kilauea fire pit. Here, after prayers, gifts and offerings, the bones were thrown into the pit. That was the way to ensure that the uhane (spirit) live always with Pele. If the body was not acceptable to Pele, it was thrown back to the priest officiating at the ceremony and was returned to the burial cave.

Family bones were sometimes kept in a little grave house near the home, or it was built over the grave. The grave house held the dead person's clothes, jewelry and keepsakes. Food was constantly supplied for the spirit.

In Ka'u, Hawaii, you can see the famous grave house that has curtains, a completely made bed, a dresser and a table on which food is placed daily. The dresser holds the clothes and personal items of the deceased.

The great fear in those days was the desecration of bones. An enemy might burn them. He might also expose them to sunlight, which was an insult. The bones might be completely destroyed, or the skull used as a spittoon. To burn or completely destroy bones meant that the spirit would never join the aumakua. It was also an insult to make fishhooks from bones, although doing so to a white man's bones was all right, and might even bring good fishing luck.

The old ways about bones still hang on. Most Hawaiians abhor cremation, but they don't mind it if a loved one is buried at sea.

Royalty were especially concerned about the desecration of bones. The funeral processions were held in secret and at night. Wailing was not allowed and often the mourners would take a devious route to the burial place.

As late as 1966, caves containing human skeletons were discovered on the Kona Coast, a favorite spot for tourists. Objects found with the bones, however, indicate that the bodies were not buried in ancient times, but fairly recently. Found were things like kerosene lanterns, pipes and burlap, items which were not known to the ancients. This cave site, and others along the Kona Coast (some forty in all), were left intact because there is a law which prevents people from disturbing them—to say nothing of what the dead can do to the living if their remains are not respected.

Reporter Chris Cook is skeptical about most matter of the occult, but yet freely admits that he had a run in with the feared "Night Marchers" that raised just about every hair on his body. (photo by Tim Beckley)

UNDYING POWER OF THE GODS

E kini o ke 'kua
Ye forty thousand gods

E ka lehu o ke 'kua
Ye four hundred thousand gods

E ka lalani o ke 'kua
Ye rows of gods

E ka pukui akua
Ye collection of gods

E ka mano o ke 'kua
Ye four thousand gods

E kaikuaana o ke 'kua
Ye older brothers of the gods

E ke 'kua muki
Ye gods that smack your lips

E ke 'kua hawanawana
Ye gods that whisper

E ke 'kua kiai o ka po
Ye gods that watch by night

E ke 'kua alaalawa o ke aumoe
Ye gods that show your gleaming eyes by night

E iho, e ala, e oni, e eu
Come down, awake, make a move, stir yourselves

Eia ka mea ai a oukou la, he hale
Here is your food, a house

In Hawaii, all gods are equally important. All of the gods together are called the *kini akua*. It is a widespread belief that one does not offend a god by not praying to him because the god's name has been forgotten. The god with the elusive name may be the one with an interest in the one who prays. Therefore, the prayer above is for all gods—and no one is slighted.

The following was told to me by an old Kahuna on the big Island of Hawaii. It's no secret. The Kahuna teach these words to all who listen:

The Almighty Keawe is the Supreme Being. Spirit energy flows from his temple of the Sun in the blue mists of heaven. The spirit energy flows through the Heavenly Father, called Kane, and the Holy Mother, called Uli. The same energy visits their three sons, who are the Princes of Heaven: Lono, Kanaloa, and Ku. The breath of life comes from their father and mother, and the three sons breathe it throughout the world so that all of God's children are given the energy to live.

LONO

Lono is considered the highest spiritual god of the Sun. He is the Savior and is worshipped as such. He is the god of the Cross, the god who came down from the Cross, the Pillar of Strength. He is the comforter of all.

The priest told me that Lono is also the god of medicine because the rays of the sun make it possible for vegetation to grow. And the natives get their medicines from herbs.

The Kahuna also said that the living things in this world are not sustained merely by food and water, but by an energy in the air called Mana. This is spirit food, the vital force of energy that if cut off would put an end to the living world.

Throughout the Polynesian world, Lono, Ku, Kane and Kanaloa are invoked in a simple chant:

> *A distant place lying in quietness*
> *For Ku, for Lono, for Kane and Kanaloa*

KU AND THE KU GODS

There are Ku and Hina, Ku being the male or husband (Kane) and Hina being the female or wife (Wahine). They are the gods of heaven and earth and control the fruitfulness of the earth and the generations of mankind.

Ku means to rise upright; Hina to lean down. The rising sun is Ku; the setting sun is Hina. When one prays to Ku, one faces east. In the afternoon, when the sun is setting, one faces west to pray to Hina.

The Kahuna I spoke to in Hawaii told me that all children are from a single stock, which is Ku. The Kahuna teaches a prayer for sickness to either Ku or Hina, depending on the position of the sun. The prayer is thus:

"Ku (or Hina), listen! I have come to gather for (the name of the sick person) this (name of the herb or plant) which was rooted in Kahiki, spread its rootlets in Kahiki, produced stalk in Kahiki, blossomed in Kahiki, branched in Kahiki, bore

fruit in Kahiki. Life is from you, O God, until he (or she) crawls feebly and totters in extreme old age, until the blossoming of time at the end. Amama, it is freed."

Ku presides over all male gods. Hina presides over all female gods. They are the national gods for all the people. There are a number of Ku gods who are worshipped to produce good crops, good fishing, long life, family and national prosperity. To have a prosperous year, one must pray:

"O Ku, Soften your land that it may bring forth. Bring forth where? Bring forth in the sea (name the fishing area), squid, ulua fish . . .

"Encourage your land to bring forth. Bring forth where? Bring forth, on land, potatoes, taro, gourds, coconuts, bananas, calabashes.

"Encourage your land to bring forth. Bring forth what? Bring forth men, women, children, pigs, fowl, food, land.

"Encourage your land to bring forth. Bring forth what? Bring forth chiefs, commoners, pleasant living, bring forth good will, ward off ill will."

The Kahuna tell us that each Ku god has his own name and the name indicates his charge. The prayer above is a general one for all purposes. Below we list the individual prayers for special needs.

Ku-moku-hali'I
Ky spreading over the land

Ku-pulupulu
Ku of the undergrowth

Ku-olono-wao
Ku of the deep forest

Ku-holoholo-pali
Ku sliding down steeps

Ku-pepeiao-loa and-poko
Big and small-eared Ku

Kupa-ai-ke'e
Adzing out the canoe

Ku-mauna
Ku of the mountains

Ku-ka-ohia-laka
Ku of the ohia-lehua tree

Ku-ka-ieie
Ku of the wild pandanus vine

Those are the gods of the forest and rain and they are invoked through those prayers. Ku gods of husbandry are invoked with the following prayers:

Ku-ka-o-o
Ku of the digging stick

Ku-kulia
Ku of dry farming

Ku-keolowalu
Ku of wet farming

Ku-ula or Ku-ula-kai
Ku of the abundance of the sea

There are four Ku war gods. They are:

Ku-nui-akea
Ku the supreme one

Ku-kaili-moku
Ku the snatcher of land

Ku-keoloewa
Ku the supporter

Ku-ho'one'enu'u
Ku pulling the earth together

There is only one Ku god of sorcery, and the English translation is startling:

Ku-waha-ilo
Ku of the maggot-dripping mouth.

HINA-ULU-OHIA

Hina is the growing ohia tree. This tree is sacred. No one on a visit to the volcano should dare to break the red flowers to make a wreath or pluck the leaves or branches during the trek to the volcano. When you are leaving the volcano area, you must produce the proper invocations before plucking the flowers. The results may be dire, with a rainstorm the least of the ills that befall you.

The worst? You may incur the wrath of Pele. Pele is a goddess with an unpredictable nature. We will delve more deeply into this subject later, but for now let us just say that a tall foreigner who came from Kahiki cultivated bananas in a marshy spot in the valley. Pele came to him in the shape of an old woman. The man refused to share his bananas with her. She punished him by first nearly freezing him to death. And while he sat all hunched over and trying to keep warm, she smothered him in a stream of molten lava.

Timothy Green Beckley

KU-MAUNA

One may scoff at the gods, but it is not wise to do so, as the late Johnny Searle learned to his horror. This story came to me from the Kahuna who knows Hawaiian lore inside and out.

He told me that Ku-mauna is the god of the mountain. And in Hawaii there is a mountain called Kumauna, where sick people are brought and left overnight to be cured. The ritual is performed with great reverence. Visitors are warned to be quiet and respectful when they are in the vicinity of Kumauna.

Johnny Searle in 1896 was not. He was riding down the valley with a party of goat hunters when he raised his rifle and shot at a Kumauna boulder. He yelled, "There, Kumauna, show me your power!" The bullet knocked off a piece of the rock. Searle took it home and threw it in the fireplace.

That night there was a cloudburst. Great stones were flung all over the backyard of Searle's plantation. The stones are still there today for anyone to see.

KANE

The name is pronounced Kan-ay. He is the leader of all the great gods. It was Kane who formed the three worlds—the upper heaven of the gods, the lower heaven above the earth, and the earth itself, which is mankind's garden.

A wise Kahuna told me that it was Kane, with the help of Ku and Lono, who created man. I was struck by the similarity between this ancient Hawaiian legend and the creation as reported in Genesis.

According to legend, Kane, Ku and Lono created their three heavens to dwell in. Kane had the uppermost heaven, Ku the next one and Lono occupied the lowest. They then created the earth to rest their feet on. Kane made the sun, moon and stars and placed them between heaven and earth.

Next, Kane made an image of man out of the earth. He used clay and red earth, which was formed in the image of Kane. Ku was the workman. Lono was an aide. When the man was finished, Kane and Ku breathed life into the male figure by blowing into his nostrils. The man rose to his feet, then knelt before the gods. He was named Ke-li'l-ku-honua. The gods gave him his own garden to live in and they called it Kalana-I-hauola. Later, the gods fashioned a wife for the first man by removing her from his right side. The first man was given a law to uphold, but he broke it, and from then on was known as "a god who fell because of the law."

KANE AND KANALOA

Kane is the waterfinder; Kanaloa is the god of the evil-smelling squid. Because of his actions against Kane, he has been equated with Satan. It is said that Kanaloa and his spirits rebelled against Kane, and were sent down to the underworld. The rebellion took place because Kanaloa's spirits were not permitted to drink awa, the drink of the gods. Kane and Kanaloa are the god and evil wishers of mankind. It was said that when Kane drew his figure of the first man in clay, Kanaloa also drew one. But Kane's came alive; Kanaloa's remained as stone. Furious, Kanaloa cursed man to die.

Kanaloa then began to make poisonous things. He seduced the wife of the first man and as a result, the first man and his wife were driven from the garden spot.

This story was so similar to the Bible and the serpent (a poisonous thing) in the Garden of Eden, with its temptation of Eve, that I could not resist asking the Kahuna if it was possible that the Hawaiians adopted the Biblical story as their own.

He shook his head soberly and said: "The legend has been passed down from generation to generation. The ancients knew of no land other than Polynesia." He reminded me that Hawaiians had no written language until the early part of the 19th Century.

Kanaloa is closely associated with the underworld that an expression in Hawaii has it that an object may be "fished up from the very depths of Kanaloa." Oddly, both gods, Kane and Kanaloa, are often coupled. Canoe men, for instance, often invoke them. Kane for canoe building, Kanoloa for sailing.

A hula song still danced today alludes to Kane's drinking of awa, the gods' drink:

Ua maona a Kane I ka awa
Kane has drunk awa

Ua kau ke kaha I ka ulua
He has placed his head on a pillow

Ke hiolani a la I ka moena
And fallen asleep on a mat

Kipu I ke kapa a ka noe
Wrapped in a blanket of mist.

SECRET LANDS OF THE GODS

The Kahuna told me that I could see these lands even today at sunrise or sunset if I looked toward the far horizon. Often these lands are touched by a reddish light. According to the will of the gods, these lands may be submerged under the sea, or float on it, or rise in the sky. "You must not point at what you see," the Kahuna warned me. "It is very bad form to do so."

Kana and Kanaloa are on these lands. So are many other gods. The area is somewhere between heaven and earth where the gods enjoy all of the fruits of the earth without labor and without death. The Kahuna told me that there is no land on earth that can compare with the secret lands of the gods.

AUMAKUA OR ANCESTORS

My informant in Hawaii, the Kahuna priest, told me that the aumakua or ancestors live in an awe-inspiring place called Po. Po can only be described as a place that knows no time, where land, sea and sky are as one. My Kahuna friend said that the aumakua were made into gods or god-spirits. And they are extremely powerful, although their earthly families are still much in their minds and hearts. When needed, these gods and god-spirits can give strength and comfort. When danger threatens, they can give warning. They can inspire an earthly craftsman to do finer work. They can encourage the athlete to perform harder feats. However, they also judge the actions of the living and are quite capable of meting out justice and punishments when necessary.

These entities are called the lesser gods. They number in the thousands. Some say that there are more gods than living people. In any event, all of these gods live in Po, which has been described as eternity, hell, chaos, darkness or obscurity. In all of the Hawaiian Islands there are only two places where one might jump off into the Po realm. One is near Kaena Point in the Waianae District, and the other is at South Point on the Island of Hawaii. The hope of all Hawaiians is to join their ancestors after death: "Please the gods during life and you will join the aumakua after death."

The problem here is that no one is certain that the dead pleased the gods during life. If not, the ghost could be doomed to an eternity of existing as a nomad, wandering forever, hungry, welcome nowhere. The Hawaiians' idea of hell is hunger.

One important purpose of the aumakua is to intercede between man and the gods. They are the mediators, the spokesmen for earthly beings. They also provide superhuman strength to mortals when needed.

There is a tale told to me by the Kahuna of a severe earthquake that occurred on the Island of Hawaii. A building collapsed on a man who weighed about 250 pounds. He was in great pain and completely helpless. His problem was that a large beam of wood lay across his legs, pinning him down.

His wife sized up the situation quickly and called upon her aumakua to help her. She weighed only 100 pounds. Nevertheless, she wrapped her thin arms around the beam and lifted it. She then moved it out of the way. Her husband recovered from his injuries.

Everyone was amazed by the feat. Later, the tiny woman tried to duplicate it, but could not move the beam an inch!

We have our own parallels. How many times have you read in newspapers about someone in a dire emergency performing acts of superhuman strength? Perhaps a car was lifted to free someone underneath. A huge stone move off a trapped person. The hero performing the act usually says that he doesn't know where the strength came from, that it was simply there when he needed it.

Perhaps we Westerners have our own aumakua who come to our rescue in times of need.

RITUAL OF DEATH

Every Hawaiian family has its own aumakua. When one dies, his family wants to be as sure as possible that he will reach their aumakua in Po. The ritual to ensure the trip is called "kakau'ai."

The flesh is removed from the body and the bones are wrapped in tapa, also spelled kapa, and is a soft Polynesian bark cloth fashioned from bast of the paper mulberry. Parts of the body, like the hair, fingernails or even the bones, are taken to a volcano or to the sea, depending on whether the family was related to the sea gods or the volcano gods.

An offering is made, usually a pig or awa, a drink for the gods, and is thrown in with the corpse. A local prophet pays homage to the particular god and prays that the dead one will be accepted into the family of aumakuas.

As we have said, not all of the dead are immediately accepted into Po. If the dead have displeased a god, he will not see Po. Also, if the relatives refuse to release the spirit by practicing "unihipili," which means holding on to parts of the dead body like the bones or the blood, the spirit will wander aimlessly. In these cases, the living are simply unable emotionally to separate themselves from the dead; they keep the body parts and deify them. These wandering spirits are called lapu (ghosts) and are greatly feared.

THE DREADED LAPU

According to my informant, lapu still frighten Hawaiians with maddening regularity. They are evil, impish. They are likely to trip you up in the dark, pinch you in bed, choke you, scare your horses, knock on your door late at night, sour your milk, frighten your baby, crumble a stone wall, send out horrendous odors, mutter and chirp in your room in the dark, and cause a weight on your chest while sleeping.

There are remedies you can use to discourage lapu from entering your room: hedges of ti leaves will do the trick, and so will glowing embers.

Apparently, they work. Recently, a woman was in an elevator in a new condominium on Ala Moana Boulevard. She was attacked and beaten by unseen forces. The next day a ti leaf was placed on the floor of each elevator. There has not been an attack since.

The best way to fight evil spirits, I have been told, is to show no fear. If you don't believe in the power of evil, it can't hurt you.

This was demonstrated at a fire station recently. A fireman was awakened out of a sound sleep because he thought he was being choked by a lapu. His friends could hear him gasping and tried to calm him down. When he told them about the lapu, they too became frightened. In fact, they assembled in one room and spent a sleepless night worried about an invasion of lapu. Still, there were other firemen who did not believe in ghosts and refused to believe that their buddy had been attacked by one. They slept peacefully all night.

Chapter 5:
Helpful Spooks, Good Spirits and Guardian Angels

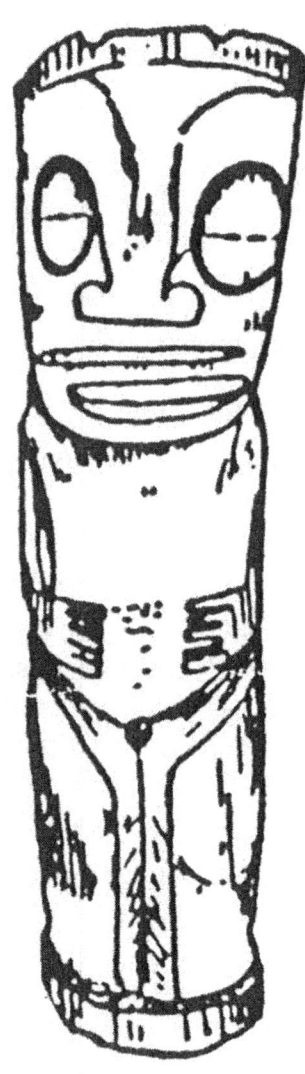

Helpful Spooks, Good Spirits and Guardian Angels

Most religions hold to the belief that we all have at least one—if not several—"guardian angels." Entire books have been written on this very topic and many are the stories of those whose lives have been saved by some friendly invisible hand from the heavenly realms.

The Kahuna take such things as helpful ghosts, good spirits and guardian angels matter-of-factly. The way the Kahuna see things, there are ample spirits of all types to go around. Some are ancestors now residing outside this world, while others are beings who have never known an existence on earth, but whose sole purpose in existing is to lend a helping hand when we need it most.

As a psychic, I know these things are real. Perhaps you will one day, when something out of the ordinary happens to you!

--Maria H. Carta

NA 'AUMAKUA, THE SPIRIT GUARDIANS

As we have said, there are a great number of gods. Among them are the aumakua. Each individual has an 'aumakua who is his personal guardian. And everyone in the individual's family has the same sort of 'aumakua. That is, if the individual's guardian is an owl, then all members of the family have guardians that are owls. 'Aumakua can also be sharks, lizards, birds or fish. In any case, no matter what the species, all members of that species are treated with the utmost of respect by the family. The spiritual relationship is so close that the family asks the species to come to feasts and festivities, and to come in times of strife. The 'aumakua are present to act as healers, advisors, to ward off troubles and to punish faults. The following is a prayer to the 'aumakua:

E na 'aumakua mai ka pa's iluna ka pa'a ilalo
O guardians from the solid above to the solid below

Ka hooku'I a me ka halawai
From the zenith to the horizon

E ka 'ai he 'awa
Here is the food and the 'awa

E 'ike la 'u ia (inoa) ka 'oukou pulapula
Take notice of me, your offspring

O ke ola mau loa no ko'u a kau I ka pua/aneane
Let my life continue till I reach extreme old age

A kanikoo, a pala lauhala
Until the cane sounds (and I am)

Kolopupu, a haumaka 'iole
Bent with age, and blurred eyes of a rat

O ke ola ia a 'oukou, e na 'aumakua
It is life by you, O 'aumakua

'Amama, us noa, lele wale
'Amama, free of taboo, flown away

GHOST OF THE RAINBOW MAIDEN

It is said that the ghost of the Rainbow Maiden can be seen by just about anyone in Manoa Valley, playing in and around the valley day or night and whenever there is a misty shower that is touched by sunlight or moonlight.

The natives have three names for her: Kahalaopuna, The Hala of Puna and the Kaikawahine Anuene, the latter meaning the Rainbow Maiden.

At one time, the Maiden had two lovers. One was from Waikiki, and the other from Kamoiliili, which is halfway between Manoa and Waikiki. Each lover wanted the Maiden's lovely rainbow arch to cover his home, and of course to have the maiden dwell inside.

Kauhi, the Waikiki chief, settled the problem quickly. He killed the Rainbow Maiden and buried her body. Fortunately, the Maiden's guardian spirit was an owl named Pueo, who was nearby at the time. He quickly dug up the body and brought it back to life.

The killing and resurrection of the Maiden occurred several times. Then Chief Kahui buried the body deep under the gnarled roots of the koa-tree. The owl-spirit dug down but was unable to bring up the body. The roots were too strong. He finally gave up, assuming that by now life had left the Maiden's earthly form.

The murdered girl's spirit wandered around with the hope that she would be restored with her body. She did not want to descend to Milu, which was the Hawaiians Under-world. This was Po, which I mentioned earlier. It was another name for Hell.

The Maiden, whom we can call Kahala, began to panic. Her body was growing cold and stiff. So she flitted about, desperately trying to attract someone's attention. She needed to have someone invoke the prayer of life.

But there was no doubt about it. The shadows of real death closed in on her. Then suddenly she saw a noble young chief nearby. He was Mahana, the chief of Kamoiliili. The girl's spirit hovered about him, trying to get his attention.

Mahana did feel a presence, a call of anguish, and he knew it was a ghost, a ghost-god, or aumakua. An unseen influence led him to the koa-tree. He saw that the earth was disturbed because of the owl's scratchings. He ripped up the roots and saw the lovely girl's body—and recognized her immediately as the Rainbow Maiden—the girl he had loved.

Mahana took the body to his home. Mahana's eldest brother was a Kahuna, who was immediately requested to invoke the prayers and chants necessary to unite the spirit and the body Kahala, the Maiden.

The Kahuna was an especially good one, but he failed. He needed help, so he called upon the spirits of two sisters. They were the aumakuas who watched over the Mahana clan. The sisters guided the Maiden's spirit to the body and persuaded it to enter the feet. While the Kahuna chanted, the sisters pushed the girl's spirit slowly up into the body. At last the soul was restored.

The young Maiden stayed at the chief's house while her health was restored. Eventually, Kahala and Mahana the chief fell in love.

But there was a problem. Chief Kauhi, who had killed the Rainbow Maiden, was still a thorn in the lovers' side. Young Mahana got into an argument with Kauhi, with the upshot being that Kauhi admitted killing the Maiden. The young chief said that Kahala was alive and living with his sisters.

The cruel chief did not believe him. He said the girl must be an imposter. In fact, he was so sure that he had killed the maiden that he offered to be baked alive if she came before him.

The noble chief thought the proposition was a good one, but the cruel chief was no fool. He was certain that Mahana would try to trick him. So he proposed a test not only for the Maiden, but for the two spirit-sisters. Kauhi knew that if there were ghosts present, the "spirit catchers" from Milu could be invoked, and the ghosts would be taken away to the spirit land and properly punished.

THE RAINBOW MAIDEN'S TEST

The cruel chief's sorcerer devised the test, which was to spread the large and delicate leaves of the ape-plant on the ground where the Maiden must walk and sit before the judges. A human would bruise and tear the leaves; a ghost would not make any impression on them at all.

If some other maiden pretended to be Kahala, her divine ancestor Akaaka would let everyone know about the deception.

The leaves were prepared. The imus, or oven, was lighted. Everything was ready.

Finally, the Maiden appeared with the spirit-sisters. Kahala had nothing to fear. She would disturb the leaves. But what of the sisters? They were ghosts. Once it was learned that they had not disturbed the leaves, the spirit catchers would come and snatch them away.

The spirit-sisters told Kahala what to do. They said that she must try to disturb as many leaves as she could with attracting notice. The Maiden did as she was told as she and the sisters slowly walked on the leaves. And the multitude that watched immediately recognized the Rainbow Maiden as the child of the divine rain and wind of Manoa Valley. There was no question in their minds—she had died and was resurrected!

Chief Kauhi was shocked. He recognized the girl he had killed again and again. In desperation he cried, "I feel the presence of spirits here, and they are somehow connected with her!"

He quickly devised another ghost test. It was thought that any face reflected in a pool or calabash of water was a spirit face. Ghosts were often discovered this way. The face in the water was grasped by the watcher and crushed between his hands, and the spirit was destroyed.

A calabash of water was brought forth. So anxious was the cruel chief to detect the presence of ghosts with the girl that he leaned over the calabash. His own face was reflected in the water! The face was his own true spirit escaping for the moment form his body. Before he could draw back, Akaaka plunged his hands into the water and crushed the reflected face with his strong hands. Thus the spirit was destroyed before it could return to the chief's body.

Chief Kauhi was then thrust into the hot oven and baked alive. All of his lands and retainers were given to the lovers, Kahala and Mahana.

Mahana, it is assumed, lived his normal span of life, but the Rainbow Maiden's spirit still lived in Manoa Valley. She still prances among the raindrops, glorying in the sunlight and moonlight that produce such striking colors in a graceful arch.

ANCESTOR GHOSTS

When a Polynesian died, the ghost crept out of the body, coming up from the feet until it rested in the eyes. The exit from the body came form the corner of one eye. It was a sort of wind body. It would move around the room and leave through any opening it found. It might perch itself in the trees like a bird, or on the roof. Or it might sit on some rocks outside the house. Finally, it might go back into the body and make it live again. If the ghost met some ancestor ghosts, it is likely that it would be led away, never to return. If that happened, it must become a member of the aumakua, or ancestor ghosts, or join some desolate ghost vagabonds.

Hawaiian families sometimes tossed their dead into the sea in the hope that the ghost would find a home in a shark or an eel. A family might cast the bones of the dead into the crater of Kilauea so that the spirit would become a flame of fire like the goddess Pele. Some ghosts went up into the sky and concealed themselves in the clouds.

Ghosts who lived in the clouds performed great services for their families. They took up residence in the gray clouds that dropped rain on the farmlands so that things would grow for their family. And if their loved ones were in trouble with an enemy, the ghost would move to the black thunder clouds and force torrents of rains and floods on the enemy.

Ghost ancestors often made their homes close to where their families toiled. There were ghosts to handle the tapa, or kapa, the calabash or the canoes. Ghosts toiled in the fields, and they were fishermen and bird hunters. They dwelt in homes or in oceans or in the air above, or even in humans. When that happened, the ghost would make the human sneeze and shake as though he had a cold, and the person was said to be an ipu, or a calabash that contained a ghost.

On occasion, a ghost could be seen sitting on the head or shoulder of the person to whom he belonged. In my talks with an elderly Hawaiian woman, she once told me that she could see a ghost-god on my shoulder, and whispering something in my ear. I must confess, though, that I heard nothing. She said the ghost took the shape of a colored light. Sometimes they look like fire.

The old woman told me that a ghost can be detected in many ways—a sibilant swishing sound or murmur, or a sensation in part of the body, like a twitching eyelid. A shivering chill meant that a ghost had touched the body.

To avoid ghosts that may not be friendly, one must invoke the following prayer:

O Akua-loa (long god)
O Akua-poko (short god)
O Akua-muki (god breathing in short sibilant breaths)
O Akua-hokio (god blowing like a whistling wind)
O Akua-kie (god watching, peeping at one)
O Akua-nalo (god hiding, slipping out of sight)
O Akua—All ye Gods, who travel on the dark night paths
Come and eat
Give life to me
And my parents
And my children
To us who are living in this place, Amana (Amen).

This prayer was designed to protect one against ghosts.

Positively the strong but not the silent type, this carved temple image stands 6 feet 5 inches high but probably appeared even more menacing because of the support that held it in place not to mention its fierce facial features and wild headdress. It stood guard by the temple as the Kahuna went about their magical practices Today it is a part of the Bishop Museum collection. (photo by Tim Beckley)

THE GUARDIAN ANGEL GHOSTS OR AUMAKUAS

The aumakuas were described as being *laka*, or very tame and helpful. If one lived in a shark, the shark would be tame. It would like to be petted on the head and would open its mouth for a sacrifice. He would be given awa or meat, and would then swim away. If an aumakua lived in a bird, the bird would be tame. An aumakua-contained owl would scratch at a grave and would bring a body back to life. An owl would also untie the bound hands and feet of a prisoner he was protecting so that the person could be free from his captor.

Altars were built for the aumakuas. They were no more than little piles of coral. A chief would build a little house for his aumakua, where the ghost could come and rest, and enjoy the offerings that were placed in it for him.

If a family member became sick, the aumakua made him well after a spotted dog was sacrificed with awa, red fish, red sugar cane and some grass. If the ghost was in a shark, then a black pig was sacrificed, a dark red chicken, and some awa wrapped in new white kapa made by a virgin. This bundle would be carried to the beach, and the following prayer offered:

> *O aumakuas from sunrise to sunset*
> *From North to South, from above and below*
> *O spirits of the precipice and spirits of the sea*
> *All who dwell in the flowing waters*
> *Here is a sacrifice—our gifts are to you*
> *Bring life to us, to all the family*
> *To the old people, who have wrinkled skin*
> *To the young also*
> *This is our life*
> *From the gods.*

The sick person would then get well thanks to the aumakua in the shark.

THE LONELY AUMAKUA

The elderly woman I spoke with was a storehouse of knowledge, especially on the subject of ghosts. She told me that a young male relative not long ago had spent the day surfing. He was in or on the water all day, and when the sun began to set, he decided to go home. When he finally turned his back to the sea, he felt someone tap his shoulder. He turned around. No one was there.

But there was someone behind him. About 200 feet from the shore, he saw a woman holding a baby. Her long black hair streamed down her back and the water was up to her waist.

The young man was incredulous. The woman looked as though she was standing, but that could not be because the water was very deep at that spot.

The woman smiled at him and waved to him with her free arm. She beckoned him to come closer. He started forward, then stopped abruptly. Something was wrong. The woman could not be standing. He backed away, shaking his head at her. The next minute, he was in his car and speeding away.

I asked the old woman if what he saw was an apparition. She shook her head. "He saw something very real. He saw the aumakua of my dead aunt, her spirit. My aunt and her baby drowned many years ago in a tidal wave. They had been swept out to sea."

The old woman nodded, tears glistening in her ancient eyes. "I know her problem. My aunt is lonely. She wanted the young man to follow her, to die in the water so that he could be with her."

A GHOST ISSUES A WARNING

The Hawaiian girl was a missionary in Africa. Although a Christian, she clung to many of her old beliefs. One night she was awakened by an overwhelming aroma of flowers. And that was strange because there were no flowers in her room and in fact there weren't any flowers nearby outside her hut.

Nevertheless, she sat up in bed and turned up the kerosene lamp. She looked at her arm and gasped. There, quite plainly, was the "nahu akua," the mark of a spirit bite! The marks looked like the bite of human teeth!

She jumped out of bed. The girl remembered her Hawaiian lore, and knew that this "nahu akua" was a warning, a message from the spirit world telling her that a loved one was in mortal danger.

She panicked. What could she do? She was thousands of miles from her home in Hawaii. How could she investigate?

Suddenly, she dropped to her knees and clasped her hands in front of her. She was a Christian; she could pray for the protection of the one who needed it. She prayed hard and long, and then fell asleep exhausted.

The next day, a cablegram arrived. It told her that her father had been accused of a serious crime and had been sentenced to death. At almost the moment of the execution, the real killer, confused by some inner urge he didn't understand, confessed to the murder. The girl's father was released.

A TV CELEBRITY AND THE GHOSTS OF HAWAII

Arte Johnson, a comedian and onetime regular on TV's "Laugh-In," has been making pilgrimages to the islands with his wife for the past ten years. He has made friends with the Kahuna and is well aware of the fact that they utilize the power of the mind to its fullest extent, enabling devotees to walk on fiery coals and perform other feats of mind-over-matter.

"We've become close to several of the practicing Kahuna," says Arte. "They have given us magical potions composed of sea salt and other secret ingredients to bless our house."

The comedian said that his wife Gisela is particularly sensitive to the occult lore and legends of Hawaii.

"The Kahuna told us that to appease the volcano goddess Pele and live safely within its domain, it is wise to take a lock of your hair and wrap it around a human bone and bury it in the ground under your house. Well, one day Gisela walked out of the place we were living in and found a bone right in front of the house. She never did find out if it was human or not, because she simply picked it up and tossed it aside. Later, when she thought about what she'd done, she went back to the spot where the bone had landed, and it had disappeared! Not wishing to bring hard luck unnecessarily on us, she went out and subsequently found another bone that she really knew nothing about. She wrapped a lock of hair around it and dug a hole and buried it in the ground on the Island of Hawaii. We have visited Hawaii about 25 times in the last eight years, and on the day we are due to leave for the mainland, there is always a volcanic eruption. Frankly, I don't know what it means."

Johnson can't help but think there is a connection between the eruption and the bone his wife idly tossed away eight years before.

Arte Johnson tells about the time some friends of his found a set of human teeth and thought they would make a good luck charm out of them. They had found the teeth in a cave and set them in a statue made out of sea rock, and had it on display in their living room.

Arte said, "My wife got frantic when she first saw them. She told our friends that they had to get rid of those teeth, to bring them back to where they belonged because the spirit of the person to whom they belonged would haunt them and bring them bad fortune.

"Sure enough, this couple had been experiencing bad luck over a long period of time. But as soon as they followed Gisela's advice, the man sold a novel and things started going really good for them."

ARTE JOHNSON AND THE MYSTERIOUS FIREBALLS

Because of their willingness to accept that which is often considered taboo, Arte Johnson says that the Kahuna have taken both him and Gisela into their confidence, and have shown them what they consider to be the relentless wanderings of the dead.

"There's a place on the Big Island," says Arte, "where you can see lights which the local natives believe to be the spirits of unworthy souls, those that have not found their way into the equivalent of the Hawaiian heaven. We've seen them many times. They're fireballs in the distance, and they travel from right to left over the harbor at Kona. They travel the same path all the time. The natives claim that in order to keep them away, you must swear at them. Well, since we started seeing them, we've learned to swear a lot."

According to the entertainer, the meandering lights will often arrive in twos and threes, and then split up before they drop below the horizon. "The natives have a name for the phenomenon. They call it 'akualele,' which means evil spirits.

Johnson admits that he's baffled. "Personally, I have no idea what they could be. The only airport in the area closes at sundown, so those lights don't come from it. And we have seen these things at one and two in the morning. There certainly remains a big question in my mind. Until I find an answer, I have to think that maybe the natives are right and that we are actually seeing ghostly apparitions. That's as good an explanation as any. Before going to Hawaii, I never thought to believe in anything along these lines, but I've since found that many of the Hawaiians' so-called superstitions have a basis in reality. For me, they've borne fruit!"

Arte Johnson is not one who gives up easily. He says he plans to keep going back to the area until he's solved the mystery.

"And when I do," he proclaimed, "I'll yell it over to you and let you know what I've discovered."

Chapter 6:
A Dire Warning

A Dire Warning

The Hawaiian countryside has to be as close to heaven as one can possibly get on earth. Such must be one of the reasons the gods of old felt so comfortable coming down to these islands.

*But there **is** evil here just as well as anywhere else—of that you can be certain. Nobody likes to talk about it, but sometimes the sense of dread is so thick you can almost cut it with a knife.*

Assuredly, there is both white and black magic afoot in Hawaii. There are, as I had sensed, prayers and chants for positive and negative purposes. The Kahuna, after all, practiced a form of paganism that is in many ways closely akin to witchcraft or voodoo.

Thinking of this sends shivers up and down my spine, so let us proceed as quickly as possible!!!

--Maria H. Carta

Pat was our driver for the day. Regularly employed by Gray Tours, Pat was used to sitting in the front of his new van and giving the identical spiel to the dozens of tourists he escorts around all week.

"What do you know about the legends of Hawaii? Can you tell us anything about the Kahuna, or have you had any firsthand experiences with anything from the spirit world?"

Our guide seemed visibly shaken. At first, he wanted to avoid the subject entirely but then settled in to tell us about a mysterious woman he had once picked up at the side of the road who appeared very haggard. Once inside his minibus, she kept complaining about how the visitors were slowly but surely ruining the ecology of the islands. At a point in the rather one-sided conversation, Pat, a Hawaiian by birth, turned halfway around to agree with a particular point the old woman was making, when he noticed—with an ample amount of shock—that she had disappeared from the back of his van. That night, the Kilauea Volcano erupted, still further testament to the fact that the great lady of the Island, Madame Pele, had shown up in the form of a person just before she literally "blows her lid."

But more on Pele in another chapter. For right now, we are concerned with vengeful spirits and nasty things that go bump in the day or night.

After a bit of prodding, our driver had his own strange experience of this type to relate.

"I was talking to the foreman of a sugar can plantation near Waipio Valley when one of his drivers was actually lifted up off his tractor by invisible hands. I swear it's true. We actually saw him suspended in the air gasping for breath."

Apparently, the man had been mocking others who claimed to have heard the sound of the dreaded "night marchers." Several workers at this particular plantation apparently had seen the tall stalks of the sugar cane move as if someone—or something—was marching through the cane . . . but no one was ever actually seen.

Pat also mentioned that he had once walked into the Bishop Museum and felt someone standing beside or in back of him. But when he turned around, he didn't see a soul. He claims it would have been impossible for anyone to have walked away from him that fast!

Risky business, wouldn't you say? That's why we've learned to carry around a figure of one of the Hawaiian gods on a chain as a good luck charm. You might want to do the same.

The Huna faith is an extremely dangerous system to toy with. It can be used to accomplish great good, but also to inflict incredible evil. The Kahuna use their power of white magic to help and uplift mankind; they also have at their disposal the ability to perform black magic on anyone they please.

When you read the 33 major orders of the classical *Hoomana* and the *Hoomanamana* practitioners, you will note that most of them deal with the black orders of sorcery rather than white. They are:

1. *Ana'ana,* the art of praying to death.

2. *Hoo-pio-pio,* the use of sorcery to bring about death as well as various magical events.

3. *Hoo-una-una,* the art of dispatching evil spirit entities on missions of death.

4. *Hoo-komo-komo,* the art of creating sickness.

5. *Poi-uhane,* mastery of the entrapping of spirits.

6. *PuleKuni,* the practicing of a large division of ana'ana in which special objects are burnt as prayers are offered.

7. *One-one-ihonua,* mastery of a special prayer service.

8. *Kilo-kilo,* divination.

9. *Nana-uli,* the art of prophesying weather.

10. *La'au lapa'au,* the healing priests who employed herbs on occasion, but who healed broken bones and other traumas almost instantly or within a few days, through prayers and certain esoteric processes.

11. *Kuhi-kuhi puu-one,* locaters or designers of temples.

12. *Makani,* a wind priesthood with powers over mystic spirits.

13. *Hoo-noho-noho,* an order of priests within the makani priesthood who were dispensatories of spirits of deceased persons, and who could induce a "sitting of the deity."

By our standards, some of the Kahuna priests could be extremely cruel. Often their ana'ana, or praying for someone's death, was an example of the punishment not fitting the crime.

At the turn of the century, for instance, there was an old Kahuna who once had great powers. In his advanced age, he did nothing but sit on a pile of mats and stare out at the sea. He lived on the southern shore of Molokai near a village. He never worked, never fished, did not tend a garden and had no visitors. His only occupation was staring at the ocean.

People had to pass his grass but kept their eyes on the path so that they would not step on a cross mark of ki leaves, which would bring bad luck.

One day a young man named Lopaka and his friends passed close to the Kahuna. Lopaka was drunk. He and his buddies had a bottle of okolehao, which was almost empty. They were horsing around when they suddenly found themselves close to the old man. All but Lopaka back away. Lopaka said he wasn't afraid of the elemakule and proved it by staggering toward the seated man with the bottle extended. He said, "Take a drink, old man, it will rest your eyes."

The Kahuna did not budge. He eyes were on the water. He sat cross-legged. His kinei and malo were of clean tapa and across his lap was a thin stick with a tuft of dog hair tied to the end.

Furious, because the old man had not acknowledged his presence, Lopaka drained his bottle and then flung it down. He grabbed the Kahuna's stick and broke it into six pieces.

Finally, the ancient moved. One long bony arm scraped up the broken pieces and lined them up on the sand. He glared up at Lopaka and said, "Each stick is a day. Tomorrow I will remove one. The next day another. When all of the sticks are gone, you will die."

Lopaka laughed. "You are closer to the grave than I am." Then he kicked the sticks and staggered away to catch up with his friends.

The story spread quickly. Lopaka suddenly had many advisors. People sympathized with his family. The youth's father went to the Kahuna to ask what he might do to make amends. The old man sat mute. There were four sticks standing in the sand in front of him.

Lopaka's mother tried to reason with the old sorcerer. Her tears had no effect on him. Three sticks were left.

The next day, Lopaka himself spoke to the old man. He begged for his life. He said he would do anything to make up for the wrong he did.

Two sticks were left standing.

Lopaka went home and told his parents not to plan for a funeral, that he was going away so that the work of the old man would not concern them. He ate a meal while his father packed a few things for him.

Two days later, Lopaka was found on the beach on another island. He was dead. A short broken stick was clutched tightly in his fist.

Hawaiian history is full of tales like this one. When a Kahuna was crossed, it could be very bad news indeed!

THE KAPU SYSTEM

It must be remembered that the Kahuna were a product of the Kapu System that existed in Hawaii before the coming of the Christian missionaries.

There were two orders of priests under the Huna System. Those of *Ku* and those of *Lono*. The Ku rituals dealt with war; the Lono with agriculture and peace. The Ku ceremonies included human sacrifices, complete with a public executioner called the Mu. His job was not only to execute kapu (taboo) breakers, but to round up victims for human sacrifice. Women were rarely used as sacrifice. Usually, prisoners of war, slaves and kapu breakers found themselves facing Mu.

The kauwa (slaves) were outcasts, despised creatures who were isolated. They were drawn upon for sacrifices if a lawbreaker could not be found. The slaves wore a tattoo on their foreheads that showed a dot, a crescent and a pyramid. The design could not be erased.

These slaves led a miserable existence. They were described as filthy beasts. If they had children out of their class, the babies' necks were wrung like chickens. A slave had to keep his head covered with tapa when he was near people of other classes. He was permitted to seek release from his curse, but he had to do it by allowing himself to be drowned. Someone would hold his head under water while chanting, "Lie still in the sea of the Lord."

A kauwa could not refuse to go to his death. The Mu beat him senseless with a club and then offered the slave up for sacrifice. If he was not killed immediately, he was placed on a waiting list and wore a gourd around his neck.

The word "kapu" means taboo or something that is prohibited, sacred, holy or consecrated. It also means "keep out," and kapu signs can be seen all over the Islands. The big problem with the Kapu system in Hawaii was that there were so many kapus that it was impossible to remember all of them. The result was that many people broke a kapu without realizing it. The punishment was severe and swift.

Women in particular had a great many kapus to remember because they were considered second-class citizens. Women were not permitted to eat pork because it was a feast food for the gods, chiefs and priests. They could not eat bananas because that was the body of the god Kanaloa. Coconuts were denied women because the coconut tree was the body of Ku. Ulua fish was also kapu for women because that fish was offered to the god Ku in his war ritual when no human sacrifice was available. Also denied women was the Kumu fish because it was used in the ceremony when the main post of a new house was erected. Women were not allowed to eat shark, whale, sea turtle, sea tortoise and the spotted stingray. All of these fish were considered a form of the god Kanaloa.

Women were not allowed to cook their food in the same house with men. Would-be mothers had to have their babies in a separate house built just for childbirth.

All industries were carried out only by men—canoe-building, the making of nets and hooks, fishing and agriculture were men's jobs. If a woman touched a tool, it was ruined.

There have been many odd occurrences in the mountain valley of Waipio. The few locals who still reside here, tell the strange story of the black dog who appeared out of nowhere just before a flash flood that all but totally destroyed the entire community (photo by Tim Beckley)

CLASS SYSTEM

Under the Kapu System, there were two classes, the aristocrats and the commoners. The spiritual power of mana was in everything, animate and inanimate objects. All men had good mana; women had bad mana.

It was taboo to change clothes with anyone, or to use a sleeping mat for anything but sleeping. One could not sit on a head pillow or put one's feet on it.

Poi had to be eaten with two fingers. Using three meant the eater was greedy; using one meant he was stingy.

There were certain days of the month when it was kapu to fish, plant or work. Those days were for worship at the temples of the different gods. Makahiki was the season in honor of the god Lono. Kapus were in abundance at that time. All those in high places reaped a nice harvest in offering-taxes from the commoners. Lesser chiefs did the collecting of animals, feathers, cloth and tools, and they were given to the king, his nobles and the high priests.

The king was all-powerful. It was he who brought mana directly from the gods. No one could touch the king, his garment or his shadow. To do so meant death.

Pigs and dogs were sacrificed when a canoe was made so that mana could enter it. Sometimes a human sacrifice was required. If the eligibles got wind of it, they fled into the forests and mountaintops.

Men with mana had to protect themselves from women or they may be defiled. Men meant light; women meant darkness. Men were strong, women weak. If a woman dared to eat a banana, it meant instant death by strangulation. The banana was created by the gods to represent men's fertility.

When a woman menstruated, she was locked up in a small room. To escape meant death. If a woman helped her, that woman was killed.

The Kapu System kept the commoners in a constant state of fear. They could never be sure when they might be subject to the whims of the aristocrats. Many of the commoners lived from the fishing successes, but the kapus here were mind-boggling. No one was allowed to ask a fisherman where he was going. His wife was not allowed to gossip or visit or entertain anyone until he came home. He was not allowed to carry bananas with him because they were unlucky for fishermen.

The commoner had other problems, especially when he was in the presence of the king. His shadow should not fall on the king. He should never be on a level higher than the king. He should never come to the king with a wet head—that could mean death. The commoner had to prostrate himself before the king, and also had to prostrate himself when he saw food and water being carried to the king's house.

A sailor on a vessel had to make sure he was not on a deck higher than where the king was standing. Once, two young princesses were caught swimming in the king's pool. Their teacher was killed for not being a better instructor on protocol.

One was not permitted to go into the doorway of a chief, or climb over his stockade, or step in his footprint even if it was hidden in the grass. Such kapus were fatal for the miscreant.

Men were put to death by clubbing, strangulation and burning. Some were stoned to death. All of the bodies were burned until they were reduced to ashes.

The Kapu System ended in 1819, but not without a fight. King Liholiho succeeded Kamehameha the Great. One of his first acts of defiance was to eat a meal with his mother. The Kapu System died, and with it many of the negative aspects of the old religion. But many were opposed to Liholiho. A priest named Kekuaokalani rallied his forces to fight the destroyers of the gods and temples.

The battle was fought on the plains of South Kona. Kekuaokalani was killed and his army fled. The Hawaiians were then ripe for Christianity, and when the missionaries arrived in 1820, the natives immediately took this new religion to their bosoms.

Hawaiian warrior wearing a mahiole, or feather helmet, and feather war cloak.

Timothy Green Beckley

Chapter 7: Chants To Avoid Possession, Evil and Misfortune

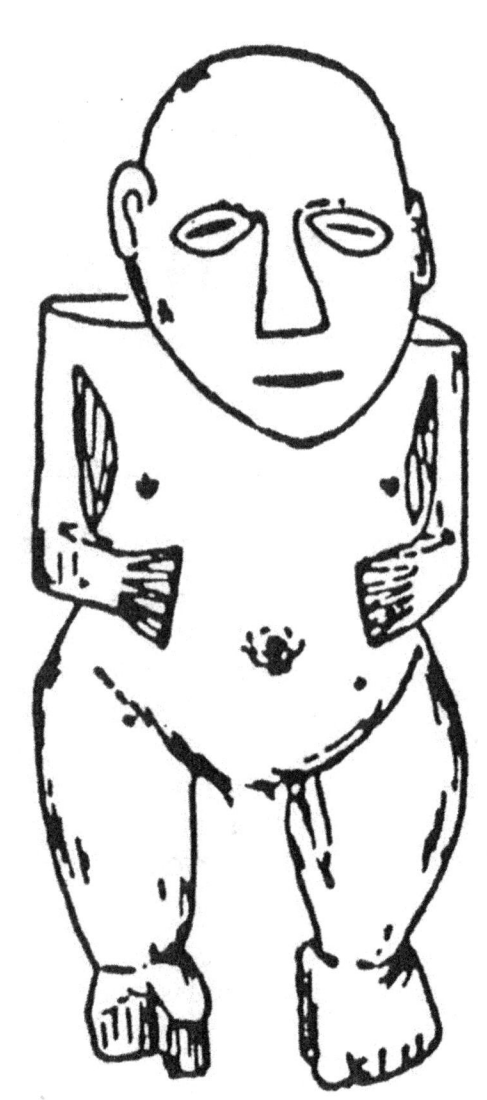

Chants To Avoid Possession, Evil and Misfortune

Doesn't it seem reasonable that if we're going to talk about evil spirits and the power they possess, we should give information on how people should go about protecting themselves from all forms of negative energy?

The chants and prayers that are given in this chapter can be utilized to protect us. They remind me of the "White Lighting" process that psychics I know use. When you feel that you are in some kind of danger, it is said that the best protection is to surround yourself with the "White Light" of God. If you are sensing that there is some kind of danger "in the air" for a loved one, you should project this white light onto this person and it will protect them. I have seen this work many times. The power of prayer is also very strong and, because the Kahuna often prayed with more than one person, it intensified the power of the prayer and helped make the chant work better.

It needs to be remembered that chanting clears and cleanses the body and soul, which, in turn, helps our psychic impressions to be stronger. This is yet another reason why we should take all the things the Kahuna believed in very seriously.

--Maria H. Carta

There are times in our lives when we feel that bad luck comes at us in one wave after another. Misfortune seems to be our lot and we are certain we are living under a dark cloud. The Kahuna remedy for a situation like this is to inform the trouble-bearing spirits and assure yourself that you have done nothing to merit such attacks. If you are innocent, the evil spirit can be ordered to return to its keeper. The Kahuna advises one to say: *"Ho' no kau me'oe,* which means, *"What you have given me, go, return to sender."* Or you can say, *"Ho'I no 'ai I kou kahu,"* which means, *"Go back and destroy your keeper."*

However, if you examine your misfortunes and discover that you have offended a god, or your 'aumakua, or a family member, or a friend, then you have a different kind of problem. Before you can hope for relief, you have to set things straight.

If you have offended a god, or your 'aumakua, you will need the services of Kahuna. If you have offended a human, the answer is much simpler. All you need to do is go to that person and seek his or her forgiveness.

This is tradition. You have to see that the offended person forgives you. If that person has placed a curse on you (the cause of your misfortune), then it has to be lifted. Not to do so is an invitation to the gods to act in the same way in the future, when forgiveness might be sought from them.

Suppose you are cursed by someone who dies before removing it? Have no fear. You can have the curse removed by going to the corpse before it is buried and saying, *"I mea ho'ola no ka mai o mea."* That means: *"Now you are gone, take all curses with you."* This is called a cutting prayer, or pule kala, and if it can't be said before the body is buried, the curse can still be lifted if you pray with a great deal of sincerity. It can also be removed by a senior member of the family of the deceased who might agree to take the curse with him when he dies.

A curse can remain in effect even if the giver dies, but it can't be inherited by the family of the person who is cursed.

There is a prayer for seeking forgiveness. It is said first, then there is an offering of 'awa. The 'awa is shared with the family aumakua and the person who gave the curse. After the 'awa has been drunk by all, food is shared by everyone present, and that includes the aumakua. The prayer is thus:

E ku I ke kala
Oh Ku, the forgiving

E Lono I kau wake kala
Oh lono who grants pardon

Weke puha ia
Giving full pardon

Kalakaua I Ahuena
Undo the knot of our sins at Ahuena

Kapu ka aha o ke makala au e Kane
Taboo is the ceremony presided over by you, Kane

Kala weke puha ia
Pardon is wide and free

POSSESSION BY AN EVIL SPIRIT

It is unfortunate if one is possessed by an evil spirit. Usually, the spirit is sent by an enemy. If one is not strong enough to fight it off, he may have to ask a family member to help him—perhaps even the entire family. In some cases, the best way to rid oneself of an evil spirit is to call in the services of a Kahuna.

The Kahuna will immediately kill and dress a white rooster and will cook it in an *imu* (oven). He then feeds the sufferer a part of the bird, telling the possessive spirit that the food is for him to eat. The spirit may then ask, but only loud enough for a Kahuna to hear, **"Heaha ka uku ia oe no kou lokomaika'l?"** *"What shall I do to repay you for your kindness?"*

The Kahuna answers: **"Hele oe l kou, a ka mea nana oe houna mai, ilaila kou hale, kau'ai, ka mea inu, kau moena; e luku I kau kahu, a kau uku is ia makou."** In English: *"Go to your keeper, the one who has sent you here, there find your home, your food, your drink, your mats, destroy your keeper and that will be your gift to me."*

The two prayers below are to be said to rid oneself of an evil spirit.

La Kane-hoa-lani, pau ko ka lani,
To Kane, Companion of the Heavens, all things of the Heavens

La Kane-huli-honua, pa ko ka honua
To Kane, Overturner of the Earth, all things of the Earth

La Kane-huli-moana, pau ko ka moana
To kane, Overturner of the Ocean, all things of the Ocean

La Ku-la-uka, pau ko uka
To Ku, there of the Uplands, all things of the Uplands

La Ku la kai, pau ko kai
To Ku, there of the Sea, all things of the Sea

La Kihe-lau'I, ke-akua hele me ke ala loa
To Stripper of Ti leaf, the deity that travels on the long road

'A'ohe 'ai, a'ohe I'a, 'a' ohe hale a kipa ai
No food, no fish, no house to be received at

Eia au la, ko kaohi pule
Here I am the chanter of prayer

Ho mai ka ike; ho mai ka mana maluna o ko kaoki pule
Extend hither knowledge, extend hither spirit power unto thy chanter of prayer

Elieli kapu, elieli noa
Profound be the taboo, profound be its lifting

Ua noa a
It is free of taboo

SECOND PRAYER

Lu'ulu'u Hana-lei I ka us nui
Hana-lei is downcast with heavy rains

Kaumha I ka noe o Alaki'I
Heavy with the mist of Alaka'I

'Oi-ku I ka loa o Ko'I 'alana
Pained by the distance of Ko'I-alana

Ke alaka'I 'ia ka malihini
The stranger is led

Hina au e palaha
I fall over, and flat

Make au I ke auka hoounauna
I die through the god of hoounauna

Ala mai au a ku a hele
I arose and stood up at the time to go

Hele au me ku'u lanakila
I went with my victory

'Aole au make I koe
I have no death remaining

O kuu akua ia I ola ai
My god through whom I live

Elieli ku elieli moe
Profound the standing, profound the lying down

Kapu o, noa
Kapu o, It is finished

PROTECTION FROM AN EVIL SPIRIT

My Kahuna friend told me to say the following prayer as a means of protection from any wandering evil spirit, or any evil spirit who may be sent to me by an enemy.

O kini o ke akua
O ye forty thousand godlings

E lehu o ke akua
Ye four hundred thousand godlings

Ka mano o ke akua
The four thousand little gods

Ka puku'I o ke akua
The assembly of the gods

Kuli mai a nana I ka'I mana'o ino
Present yourselves and behold the strides of these hostile gods

I ke kiei ana I ka mana'o ino
Guard against their evil plans

I ka nana anai I ka uhane ino a ka poe'e
Keep watch of these evil spirits of the night

Elieli kapu, elieli noa
Finished the taboo. Finished. It is free.

Amama, ua noa
The taboo is lifted, removed.

PROTECTION AGAINST THE FEARED ' ANA' ANA

There is a prayer—'Ana'ana—in which one seeks the total destruction of an enemy. It is not politic to include it in this chapter, since we are dealing only with prayers that are invoked to protect yourself from evil.

If you feel the impact of the troublemaking prayers of an enemy, you can make an attempt to return the evil to him. Prompt action may negate the need of Kahuna. The prayer below is your defense against Ana'ana, or praying to death. Allegedly, the prayer sets up a barrier that is impossible to break.

This same prayer can also be used against ho'opi'opi'o, a fiendish form of sorcery in which the practitioner touches a part of his own body and causes an injury to his victim's body in the same area.

The prayer can be said by either the victim or a Kahuna. If a Kahuna does the invoking, the victim should say things make offerings of 'awa, black pig or red fish. If the victim says the prayer, he should be away from home. He must eat, sleep, and change his clothes before returning home.

You will note that in the prayer, the victim's body is like a house that he seeks to protect, part by part.

Nan I ka pou kua
Look at the back row of house-wall posts

I ka pou alo
At the front row of house-wall posts

I ke kauhuhu
At the ridge pole

I ke kua'iole
At the upper ridge pole

I ke kunakuna
At the side post of the door frame

Ka lapauila
Also at the other side post of the door frame

I ka paepae
At the platform at which the rafters rest

Ka pou hana
The set in the middle of each end of the house

Ka uia I ka lani
The lightning in the heavens

Ka ho'I kua
Thunder in the heavens

Ka ho'I kua
The return from the back

Ka hoopa'a
The making fast

La'I kau 'a'I
Ti leaves on the neck

Ku makaha I ka lani
Stands as a sluice gate in the heavens

Malaila 'e ho'ea mai ai na hua'olelo
There will arrive the words

Ka-hiki a Lono la kau ai
Ka-hiki of lono in place.

A QUICK-ACTING PRAYER AGAINST EVIL

It has been said that the warrior Namakaokapaoo was about to be slain by an enemy armed with an axe. The enemy's name was *Pu'alii*. The warrior quickly invoked the following prayer. Pu'alii raised his axe to strike the warrior, but the weapon slipped and fell on Pu'alii, killing him instantly.

The lesson is that no matter how immediate the danger, your innocence and fast action will likely avert a tragedy if the prayer is invoked with haste.

Aloha wale ka maka o a'u wahi paoo
O how I long for the eyes of my little fishes (paoo)

E hapupuu a hapapaa mai nei
For which I am undecided, wavering

E ai paha, e waiho paha
Whether to eat, or whether to leave

O ku'u wahi aikane keia
That is my little friend

O Namakao kaia ke'lil nui o Hawaii
Namakaokaia, the great chief of Hawaii

E hee la, e hee ka hohewale
Vanquished, yes, vanquished is the coward

O kanaka no me ka ihe
The man with the spear

O ka ihe no me ka pahu
The spear and the drum

Make no is Namakaokapaoo
Shall be vanquished by Namakaokapaoo.

Crowned with the image of a golden plover, Koleamoku (the god of healing) was one of the many Ki-Akua (temple images) which symbolized helpful spirits who were the ancestors to the worshippers. (photo by Tim Beckley)

ATTRACTING A DEPARTED SPIRIT

Sometimes when a person dies there is an attempt to by a family member or lover to return the spirit to the body. It can also be done by a special Kahuna, one who is adept at attracting spirits.

There are certain lures. One is to use sweet-smelling plants like *mokihana*, *maile*, *'iliahi*, or *'olena*. These plants are wrapped around the body. Personal items are brought into the room—items which the deceased was fond of.

When the Kahuna contacts the spirit, he must lead it back into the body. Often the spirit is reluctant to return. But a strong Kahuna can use force, and he does it by urging the spirit to enter the body through the big toe. Some say the arch of the foot is the place of return. In any case, the soul of a man is forced through the right foot; the soul of a woman through the left foot. When the spirit is in the foot, the dead body is messaged, working from the feet upward. At this time someone should hold the big toe so that the spirit cannot slip out again. When the dead person is brought to life, he must take a purifying bath in the ocean and then sit down to a feast with his family and friends.

Kanahi used the following prayer to restore life to Ka'ina-li'I:

Lani pipili I ka maka o ke akua
Heaven-high one who adheres to the eyes of the god

Lani 'oaka I ka maka o ke ahi
Heaven-high one that flashes in the source of fire

Hui papa-nu'ui ka maka o ka uila
The group of highest royalty unites in the source of the lightning

Lani ki'ei a halo I ke kihi o ka malama
Heaven-high one that peeps and peers at the beginning of the month

E ho'iho'I ai ka 'uhane kino aka wailua o ke
Return hither the spirit of the shadowy body of the deceased maiden

Wahine u'I la 'e moe I ka moe niau ninouiolo ni'o
Beautiful, stately woman that lies here in the sleep of no return at the summit of the going of the taboo

O Niolopua I ke ala ko'I ula a Kane
Handsome one in the rainbow-hued mist cloud of Kane

E la a'e 'oe a.
O arise thee.

AN INVITATION TO THE DEAD

A dead body is prepared for burial only after it is certain that death has come and after all of the grieving is finished. All the food that the deceased was fond of is taken to the burial site with the body. Then a loud call is made to the ancestors: **"(Iona) eia mai kou mano."** *"(Name) here comes your descendant."*

The body is placed in the ground with the head toward the east and the feet toward the west. The corpse is then told, **"E (Iona) 'eia no 'oe hele 'nei! Hele no 'oe hele loa!"** *"Go, and be gone forever!"*

On occasion, the wish of a survivor is that the spirit must not be sent away completely. He or she will say: **"E hele 'oe a I mana'o e 'I mana'o, e ho 'I mai no!"** *"Go, but if you would like to return, come back! Here are vegetables, food, fish, clothing!"* The spirit therefore is invited to return as a guest and provide protection, revenge, and other needed services for the loved one.

After the burial, sandalwood may be burned and a prayer invoked.

Aloha na hale o maua in makamaka 'ole!
Grief for our home without our friend!

E huli au ana I makana ia 'oe, a-a-a!
I am seeking a gift for you, alas!

Aloha wale, e (iona) kaua, a-a-a!
Boundless love, O (name) between us, alas!

Timothy Green Beckley

Chapter 8:
Foretelling the Future and Other Occult Powers

Foretelling the Future and Other Occult Powers

As a psychic who practices my profession fulltime, I can fully understand why the Kahuna put such a great deal of emphasis on foretelling the future. Knowing what lies just around the bend is of interest to us all, rich or poor, famous or not. I have clients who from all over the world visiting and writing me. They are all extremely anxious to have me peer into the future on their behalf. They want to know what aspirations will be fulfilled and what pitfalls might befall them. And, of course, if anything of negative origin should be blocking their path, they would like to have the problem resolved before it takes hold firmly. The early Hawaiians were no different in their quest for spiritual knowledge that would let them lead a better life. They went to their priests for extrasensory advice, just like people come to me because they think I have the ability to know what is about to happen to them.

The "tools" of my trade include such "devices" as the Tarot cards, rune stones, astrology and numerology. The Kahuna had their own means of divination, including cloud gazing, the picking up of vibrations from human and animal bones, as well as the use of the stars, which they believed could reveal much about a person's individual fate.

As I stood in the middle of a crowd of shoppers in Honolulu, I could pick up many sensations in the air. I knew the Kahuna were very powerful magicians and probably amongst the best fortunetellers who ever lived!

--Maria H. Carta

The Kahuna consider it important to see into the future for two reasons: 1. So that they may prepare themselves for what is certain to come without fail, and 2., To change the things that can be changed.

I was told about a Kahuna named Popolo who was able to look into a calabash of water and receive messages from the gods. The visions came to him while he uttered the following prayer:

Kanikau a'e no ka Olopana
Olopana laments

Aloha 'ino no ka makua
Great love has the parent

E noho I ke ao malama
To dwell in the light of day

Aloha 'ino no ho'I au
Great love have I

I hele ho 'okahi mai nei
Who came here alone

'A 'ohe lua 'a'ohe kolu
Not two, not three

'A 'ohe kanaka a pono ai
No persons would be suitable

Lehulehu aku I ke alanui
They were multitudinous in the road

Ke ulakahi I pa-ki-wai
The one way that splashed water

He 'ihi lani la he kala'ihi
A sacred heaven high one is a long vine

O ke 'ano meha la ua pau
The awesome loneliness is ended

Ka walania o ku'u akua
The torment of my deity

Ha'awina mai ke aka o Kane
To give reflection of Kane

I ku iluna o ka honua 'aina
They stood above the earth of the land

I ke alo o'u nei la
In my presence here

Amama
Amama

Hawaiians live close to nature. They are constantly aware of changes in wind, clouds, rainbows, animals and the flight patterns of birds. They are also believers in life after death. I have spoken to well-educated people on the Big Island who told me that their dead relatives are now *aumakuas* (souls who have entered the spirit world) and that these souls have not really left the *'ohana* (family) hearth. They communicate with the living by advising, warning and instructing.

Portents also come to Hawaiians in dreams, visions and in voices from the other side. A sudden chill, a prickling of the scalp, or a feeling of déjà vu would be enough for one to seek the advice of a Kahuna, or one's aumakua.

THE KUNI RITUAL

In some cases, sorcery is blamed if someone becomes critically ill or dies. The first thought then is to reverse the spell. The victim's hair, fingernails and clothes are burned. The ashes are scattered in the direction of the one suspected of indulging in sorcery. If the chants and prayers are effective, the sorcerer is killed. If the sorcerer is unknown, his face may appear in the flames of the fire that burns the victim's possessions.

DIVINATION

A Kahuna *kilokilo* was a diviner. A warning of a coming death usually reached him first in the form of a vision. He saw that person who was about to die, perhaps in a dream, or in water. In any event, the Kahuna knew that the only way the individual could survive would be for him to perform the ceremony of *kala*, or atonement, for him.

The ceremony might include the offerings of a variety of fish, a white dog, a white fowl, 'awa, and sheets of kapa. When those items were collected, the Kahuna kilokilo lighted a fire, marking the opening of the ceremony. While the food was being cooked, prayers were offered for forgiveness. The Kahuna, the individual who was threatened, and everyone else in attendance, ate the food. If this ritual was successful, the Kahuna announced that the individual would not die.

The Kahuna kilokilo's advice was always sought when building projects were about to take place, or other important enterprises. He was a foreteller of the future. Kings sought his counsel to learn if they were about to die or have their rule overthrown.

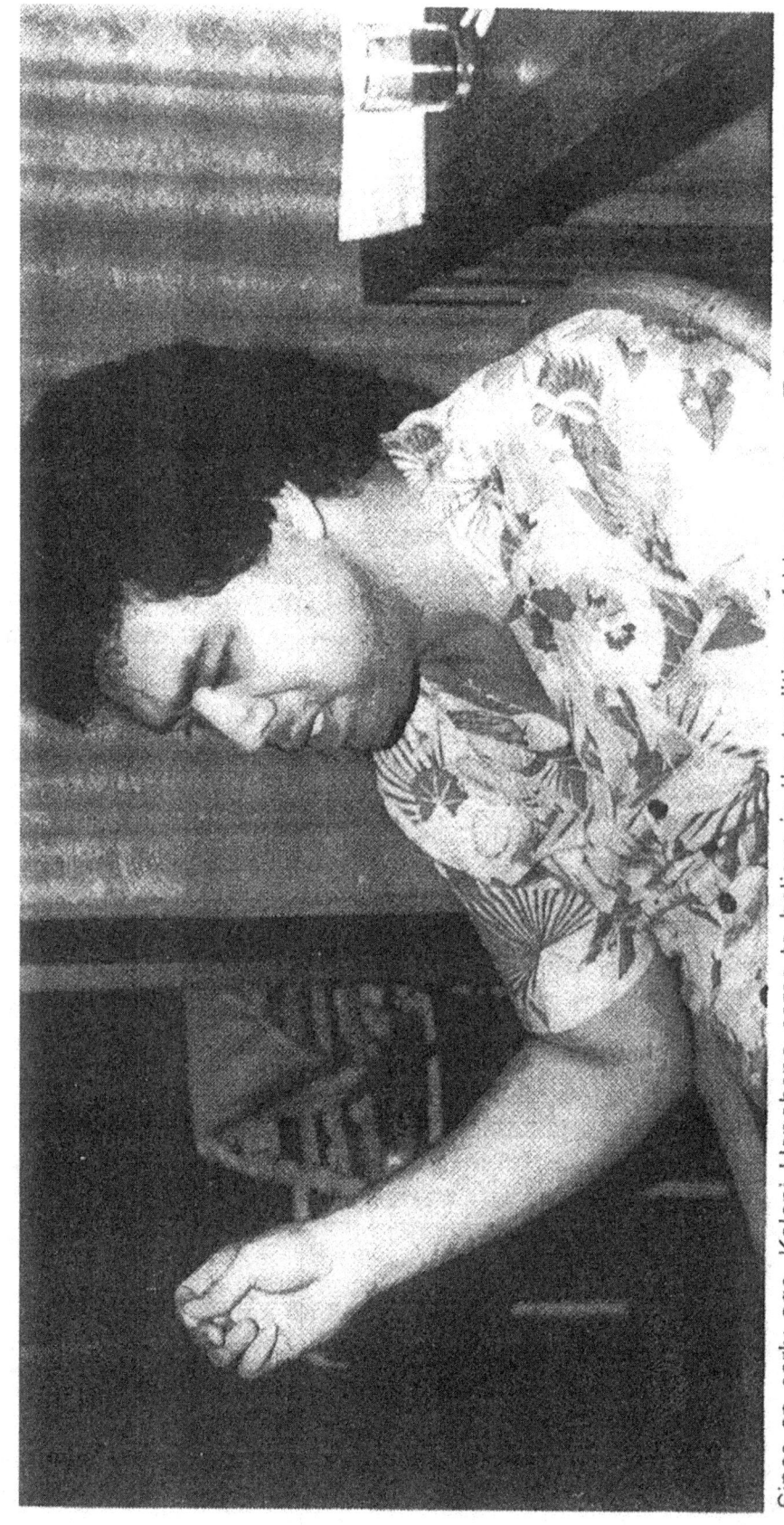

Since an early age, Kalani Hanohano came to believe in the traditions of his ancestors. Today, he is among the most knowledgeable experts on the folklore of the islands. For several years he published FULL MOON, a respected journal read by scholars and laymen all over the world (photo by Tim Beckley).

THE STARS AS AN OMEN

A star called Kane was visible only to the Kahuna kilokilo. It sometimes appeared above the moon, and was known to be a portent of the death of the king. When that star appeared, the Kahuna promptly told the king about it, and thereafter the royal monarch was guarded closely and stayed close to home. The Kahuna kilokilo was also adept at predicting disasters by looking at the position of the stars. Those who contemplated traveling a great distance often consulted a Kahuna kilokilo first to see if there were dangerous days to avoid.

PORTENTS IN CLOUDS

Cloud formations had many meanings, and the only one who could read them properly was the Kahuna kilokilo, who was sometimes called an astrologer. Kings in particular relied heavily on the wisdom of these high priests, not only in life and death matters, but in decisions concerning affairs of state.

By reading clouds, the Kahuna could also tell what the weather would be. The procedure was to wrap himself in tapa and spend hours scanning the skies. If clouds were long and narrow, rain and wind were coming. If they pointed up, the weather would be calm. If a cloud was seen lying smoothly over a mountain, it foretold rain. An overcast sky with no wind meant a thunder and lightning storm. A rainbow seen with the rain meant a short rain, but if there was wind with the rainbow there would be long sessions of rain. Big raindrops meant a short rain; small raindrops meant a long rain.

A blue sky at sunset meant a high surf. A small ring around the moon signified the arrival of large schools of fish. A large ring meant a storm was brewing.

The Kahuna priest had profound knowledge. He was the *kilokilo*. He knew how to blend his keen intuition with psychic prescience to predict catastrophic events such as wars, volcanic eruptions, tidal waves, earthquakes, droughts, famines or violent storms. Often, he needed only to study the cloud formations above his head.

In my studies on this phenomenon, I came across an article written by a brilliant Hawaiian scholar named Mary K. Pukui and published in the June 1932 issue of "The Friend." The title of the article was "Ka Makua Laiana, or Stories of Father Lyons."

According to the story, two horsemen riding toward the house of Father Lyons saw a rainbow above his home and a coffin-shaped cloud suspended by chains. The cloud rose and fell swiftly, as though manipulated by invisible hands. One of the horsemen, who had the psychic ability of a kilokilo, noted that this weird cloud formation was an omen of death. They sped to the house and learned that the master had died.

Another more recent case occurred in the spring of 1972. Two men were driving toward the city from a ranch near Pearl Harbor. The driver of the car suddenly cried out, "Look up there! Good God, it's a mo'o belching flames!" A mo'o is a great lizard in Hawaiian mythology.

Both men stared at the pink cloud that was about a half mile high. It was shaped perfectly like a standing lizard and its mouth did appear indeed to be issuing large flames.

The driver was extremely worried. His wife was due to arrive that morning on a flight from San Francisco. The plane had already been delayed a week.

This worried man was not an "ignorant native." He had graduated summa cum laude from a great Western institute of learning. He was urbane and sophisticated. Yet the evil sign was in the clouds, and he wondered if his wife's delay had anything to do with the cloud lizard. The creature was bad luck for women. The sight of one of these reptiles had to be avoided at all times; for if a woman saw one it was advisable for her to go to a Kahuna to neutralize by rituals the baneful influences. In such cases the Kahuna made his offerings to the mo'o god.

The driver's hands were gripped on the steering wheel. He said, "I have great fear for my wife."

When the woman arrived that day she was in poor health. Two months later she was dead.

THE DEAD "SPEAK"

The eyes of the dead were watched closely because they told the living important things about the soul. If the eyes suddenly opened several hours after death, it meant that the corpse was looking for someone. This was especially true if a relative died soon after; it meant that the corpse had been looking for that person. Eyes that teared after death meant that the corpse had great affection for the living. If the body suddenly became heavy while being carried, it meant that the soul did not want to leave.

THE DEAD LIVE AGAIN

Astral projection was known to the Hawaiians since the dawn of their history. They may have perfected the phenomenon to a greater degree than Westerners because they had the ability to project parts of the body, or all of it, at will. In the Huna system, astral travel is dependent upon how much of the low, shadowy body one opts to project. The point is, that if only a small portion of the body is projected, the center of consciousness remains with the physical body. Should the entire shadowy body be projected, the thickish thread of the shadowy substance known as the astral cord is the only connection between the astral body and the physical body. And even when a distant place is visited, the cord is still connected.

A Hawaiian student of psychic matters revealed that he had two out-of-body experiences, both of them apparently involuntary. He stated, "In both cases I floated out of my body to the ceiling and looked down to see my physical shell lying as though dead on the bed. The sensation was euphoric and blissful beyond my powers to describe. Each time only by a supreme effort of will power I forced myself to return. I felt that my life's work was not yet finished. I deeply regretted the fate of having to go on living in my earthly shell."

A woman named Kalima from Kona died and mourners gathered for a final viewing of the body. She took a deep breath and opened her eyes. Later, she told her family: "I died, as you know. I seemed to leave my body and stand beside it, looking down on what was me. I gazed at my body for a few minutes, then turned and walked away. I left the house and the village and walked on through village after village filled with smiling and happy people.

"At last I reached the Volcano. The people there were happy like the others, but they said, 'You must go back to your body. You are not to die yet!'

"I cried. I tried to stay, but they drove me back. Back over the sixty miles I went, weeping, followed by those cruel people, till I reached home and stood by my body again.

"I looked at it and hated it. Must I go and live in that thing again? I rebelled and cried for mercy."

THE POWER OF THE AWAIKU

I'm told that no Kahuna is needed when the *awaiku* are present. The awaiku are similar to Christian angels. They watch over the good people on Earth. Injustice and deviltry perpetrated by the unrighteous are stopped dead by the awaiku who stand ready to shield their charges at all times. A person in trouble, if he is righteous, knows that an awaiku will fly to his side to rescue him or lead him to safety.

Like Christian angels, the awaiku listen to the petitions of the children who pray to Kane and convey the messages to that god. They are the messengers. They pour out Kane's love to the faithful. They are the rainmakers who shower rain on crops that need it. They are the handlers of lightning bolts during tempests commanded by storm gods. They are healing angels who help the Kahunas by causing the divine healing power to flow from above into the spiritual healers, giving them the power to cure their patients.

STRANGE PROPHECY

At the close of one of the Makahiki festivals, the god Lono was placed in a canoe and sent back to Kahiki. Lono promised to return. A certain man, seeing this, said: "The God will depart. He will return in a small container and the people will not know him or recognize the language he speaks."

No one knows the man's name. Nor is there any way to guess the period in time when Lono was cast off in a canoe. However, in April 1820, missionaries were given permission to land at Kailua, Kona. As a good will gesture, they presented Liholiho, King Kamehameha II, with a large Bible. It was an ordinary family Bible, which pious New Englanders used to record marriages, births, deaths, and other important events in a family. It did look like a black box closed with a gold clasp.

Liholiho was pleased but puzzled. When he opened it, he found that the small characters were meaningless to him. The Reverend Hiran Bingham promised that he would teach the king how to read.

When Kahuna high priests saw the Bible, they were certain that the prophecy handed down through the ages had finally been fulfilled. And in every way. The gift was the "container" and no Hawaiian could recognize the letters of the language in which it was printed.

After the death of Kamehameha I, the Hawaiians had destroyed their own gods. To them, the god Lono answered the description of the Christ as reported by the missionaries. The Hawaiians noticed that the missionaries spent hours reading and praying over their Bible, so it was natural for them to conclude that the "black box" contained the missionaries' god. They also reasoned that the unknown letters contained the *mana*, or spirit, of this God. And they knew that if they were to learn the mysteries of God, they would have to know how to read, which they did—and became the most literate people in the world.

THE KAHUNA SPIRITUALISTS

The study of life after physical death was undertaken by a group of special Kahuna who had an inner spiritual sight that enabled them to envision what happened at the precise stroke of death—at the moment the second body (astral) rose from the lifeless body and took the soul with it. The Kahuna spiritualists were able to project their superhuman psychic senses into the astral world and see what life was like in the four main planes of the spirit world. These planes were where disembodied spirits dwelt after leaving the Earth. What the spiritualists learned was never revealed except to other Kahuna in the "inner circle."

THE COCONUT WIRELESS

The ability of thought transference over great distances was perhaps the most astounding of all the occult phenomena found in the Islands. Kahunas who had the ability were able to flash messages to other Kahunas on distant islands and receive messages back on what was called "the coconut wireless system." Long distance healings were quite common.

Earlier we said that when a Kahuna wished to make contact with someone far away, he forced his subconscious mind to send out a thread of shadowy stuff called Aka, which connected itself to the subconscious of the person he wished to contact.

With this principle in mind, it is more understandable that such adepts of ESP would be successful. The missionaries, however, were absolutely amazed by the occult phenomenon, and the term "coconut wireless" came from them. Although Westerners have been told in general how long-distance ESP works, they have not been given the specifics. To this day the coconut wireless system remains a mystery.

PROPHETIC DREAMS

Many Hawaiians still consider dreams to be a very important part of their lives, although they are somewhat reluctant to admit it. The world of old Hawaii was filled with good and bad spirits. The aumakuas (ancestral gods) and the awaiku (guardian angels) often found it easy to reach the living through dreams. It was much less frightening that way, and it also ensured the undivided attention of those who needed a warning or advice.

The dreamer does not really know what his dreams mean. In the old days, he might consult a Kahuna. Today, even though Kahunas are not easily found, there are still wise elders who are able to interpret dreams accurately.

Some Hawaiians believe that each person has two spirits, one that functions when you are awake, and the other while you sleep. That's why in Hawaii it is dangerous to awaken someone out of a sound sleep; his spirit may be wandering somewhere in search of dream material. It is proper in Hawaii to permit the sleeper to wake up naturally.

If the sleep spirit has a dream that needs to be presented to the sleeper, he must use the spirit hole (*lua'uhane*) that is located in the outer corner of the eye or a tear duct.

Some of the dream meanings may appear to be contradictory. Bananas, for instance, represent bad luck for a fisherman. But they are also a symbol of wealth, as are a bunch of coconuts.

Dreaming of a lizard is a good omen because it may tell the dreamer that his aumakua is near.

To dream of having your hair fall out, or of getting a haircut, is an omen of lost virility. If a woman dreams of losing an eyelid, she will soon lose her virginity.

To be buried alive in a dream indicates that the dreamer will have a birth experience. A tooth extraction means a death in the family. Another sign of death in a dream is the presence of birds flying in the house.

If you see in a dream a bowl of poi fermenting and overflowing, you can expect a thief to be exposed. Being trapped in a cave with no way out indicates lunacy. If you see someone wearing black or a lilac, it is a sure sign of death.

If in a dream you look at the right side of your body, you are looking at the moral side; if you dream of looking at the left side, it indicates immorality or inferiority.

To see your own shadow in a dream is to see your worst side.

If you are crawling in a dream you are expressing a desire to return to your childhood.

Dreaming of disembodied fish eyes tells us that you are looking for perpetual affection.

The body is made up of a series of fives—five fingers, five toes, and the head, two legs and two arms equal five. To dream of the number five, therefore, is a good sign.

To see a crater or a hole in a dream means death. To see in a dream a volcano means repressed passions or impulses erupting to the surface.

Dreams about salt water tell you that death for someone close is near. Sweet water in a dream means that a sick person will be cured.

Dreaming of a Koa tree is lucky. It means wealth is coming your way. To see a canoe in a dream is a bad omen.

In Hawaii, it is bad luck to change clothes with someone. If you should dream you are changing clothes with someone, it indicates that you are trying to change your ways or your nature.

To dream of ashes reveals that you will be humiliated or belittled. Vermin in your house warns of an unwanted pregnancy. A man who dreams of a burning house can expect to have a spat with his wife. Flying a kite in a cemetery means life midst death. A dream of cannibalism tells you that someone is taking another's ideas or mana.

Dreaming of a moon is not good; a new moon means magic, but the wise men don't way what kind—black or white. A full moon means madness.

Traveling in a dream foretells death, as does seeing a person asleep.

Meeting a squid or an octopus in dreamland means a possessive and clinging mother.

Are you afraid of life? Do you retreat from it? That may be the case if you dream of yourself as being dead.

If you dream of being saddled with a great weight on your shoulders, and one that you can't get rid of, you may be harboring resentment because of having too much responsibility.

Seeing an earthquake in your dreams means that your life will be disrupted.

A butterfly functions as a symbol of freedom and happiness. In other cultures, it means a departed soul has taken flight.

If you have a desire to get rid of some of your responsibilities, you may dream of seeing a baby being passed from one pair of hands to another.

It's lucky to dream of mangos. It means a prosperous year ahead.

TWO PEOPLE WHO SHARED A NIGHTMARE

The Hawaiian boys had been hunting wild boar in the Ka'u district on the Big Island. They killed one and brought it home to the family in their jeep.

They were exhausted from their long day's hunt, but oddly enough they couldn't sleep. The younger boy especially had trouble.

Then about midnight the family was awakened by a horrible scream that came from the younger boy's throat. His relatives rushed into the room to find him racing about madly, screaming and looking at his hands. He kept wiping them on his shorts to clean them while screaming about boar's blood.

The other boy was still asleep, but only until his younger brother leapt on him and clutched him tightly, begging him to help him to escape from the fangs of the boar. Then the other boy began screaming, and the two of them, with their arms locked, huddled in a corner of the room, their eyes wide with fright, their bodies soaked with sweat.

The relatives awakened the boys gently. When they were calm and able to talk, they both gave the same story, that in their same nightmare the disembodied head of the boar floated over their bed and accused them of its murder.

The youths took no part in the luau the next day.

According to the Kahuna who befriended me with exciting tales, it was not unusual for people to share the same dream. Women often claimed to have a spirit lover; men made the same claim. The spirit lovers visited only at night and allegedly had great adventures together. If a woman had a baby that looked like a fish, or some other animal, or the fetus miscarried, it was explained as a spirit baby.

Timothy Green Beckley

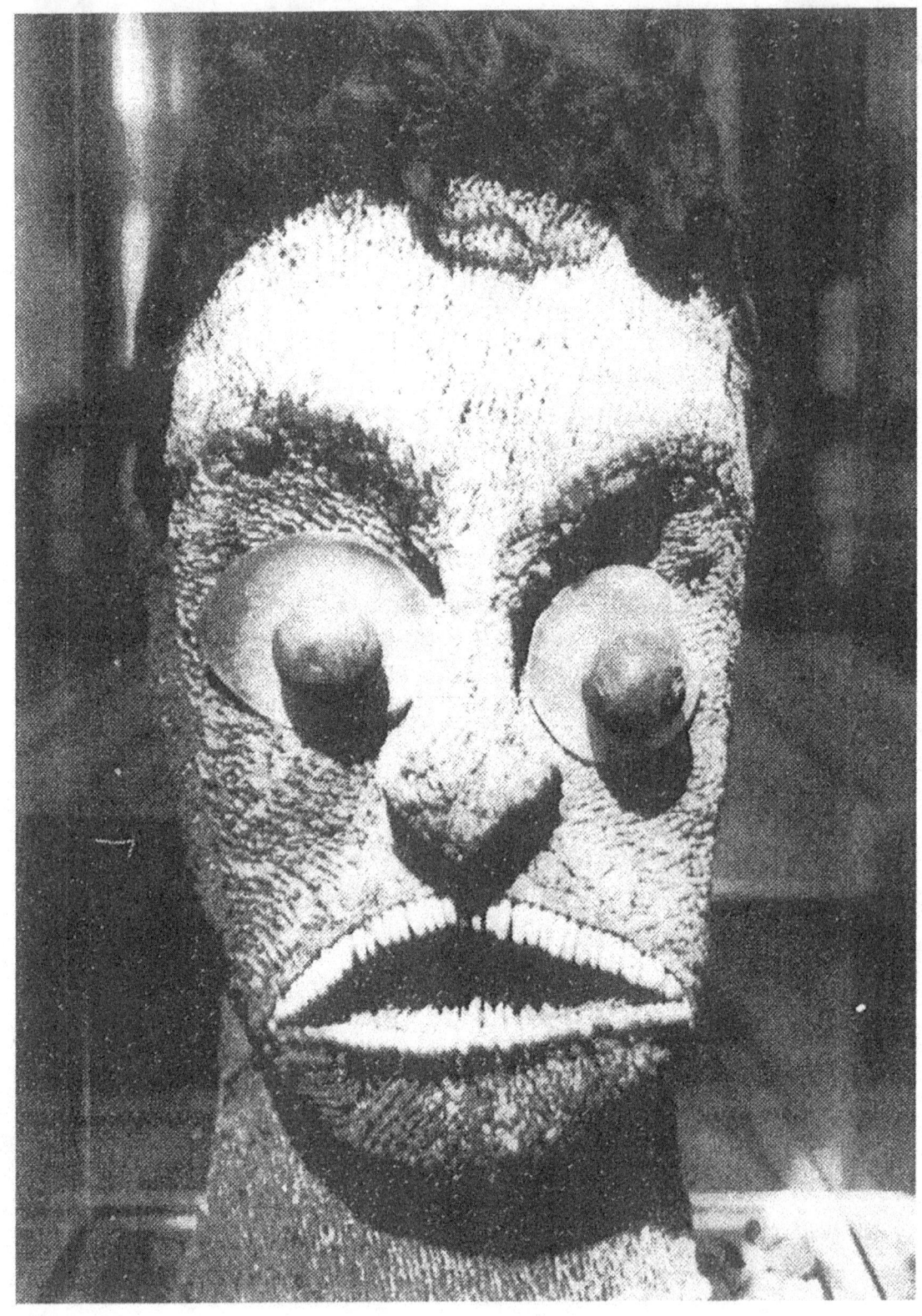

Chapter 9:
Animals and the Spirit World

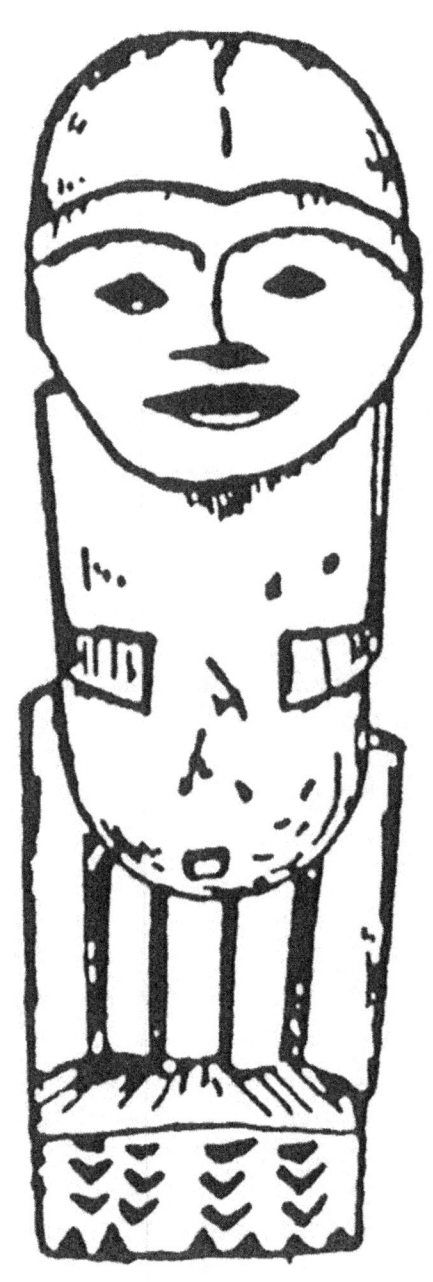

Animals and the Spirit World

On the Islands, animals are highly revered. You will seldom see anyone kicking a dog or intentionally hurting a cat, a bird, or even a small animal. The reason is that the Kahuna have long taught that animals of "every kind" are very important in nature's scheme. They believe that friendly spirits can inhabit the souls of a pet or even a wild beast. Unless it is for food, you will not find many native Hawaiians who enjoy hunting as a sport—especially not if they adhere to any of the old customs taught by their ancestors. This would be thought of a sin. And besides, how could you harm or kill an animal that might be trying to save your life?

We heard several cases of this type, including one involving a "stray" dog that wandered into Waipio Valley barking day and night just before a flash flood struck that caused much damage. The locals believe they would not have taken notice had they not remembered the tales of such "spirit animals" as told by their forefathers. As it turned out, many residents had to climb to the roofs of their homes or they would have perished. They feel that if it had not been for the strange black dog (who vanished immediately before the storm), they might have all drowned. They admit that they would not have been too concerned over the approaching dark sky, which normally they would have taken to have been just another tropical downpour.

--Maria H. Carta

Animals are acutely aware of impending disasters. That is a scientific fact that we have learned recently; the Hawaiians have known it for centuries. Before any natural disaster like an earthquake, volcanic eruption or tidal wave, animals warn us by becoming extremely agitated. They might run around in an erratic pattern, bark furiously, or even run off in fright. Sometimes their hackles rise and their eyes become dilated. Dogs always howl when death is coming. Owls have a certain cry for the same reason.

Animals also helped in more positive ways. There is a story told to me by an old man in Oahu who said that he once knew an elderly lady with the biggest heart of all. She was a poor woman who always shared what little she had with anyone who needed help.

Faithfully every morning she took a basket and went to a certain section of the beach to look for opihi (shell fish) that clung to rocks. One day she squatted on a flat rock out in the water but saw no opihi. But she was patient. She pried the rocks and still found nothing.

Then suddenly, the rock she was on started to move. She looked down and discovered that what she was on was not a rock at all but a turtle's back. She froze, not daring to move in case she slipped off. Eventually, the turtle took her to an area where the opihi were plentiful. After she filled her basket, the turtle returned her to her original spot.

ANIMAL GUARDIANS

As we stated earlier, the aumakua, or spirits assigned to help the living, take the bodies of certain animals and inhabit them. The beasts most often selected by the aumakua are the shark, the owl and the lizard. The family that adopted a creature as its aumakua would not eat it or abuse it. The animal was the family's guardian, and in many cases the dead bodies in the family were given to the animal (if a shark) to eat to appease it.

One time a woman was grasped by the ankle by a shark that was her family guardian. She screamed out its name and the shark released her, making his apologies before he swam deep into the sea.

Shark guardians were especially helpful to its adopted family because it would drive fish into the nets and would also ward off evil.

Geckoes (lizards) were fiercely loyal to families that adopted them—and they were unfriendly to the family's enemies.

The flight of the owl is watched in Hawaii for an omen of good or evil. Families on the Islands who call an owl an aumakua treat the bird with great respect.

Timothy Green Beckley

HAWAII'S KING OF THE BEASTS

Believe it or not, the king is the pig. The Polynesian settlers in Hawaii brought three edible animals with them—the pig, the dog and the rat. Although cannibalism was not unknown in Hawaii, it is believed that it would have become a way of life if it had not been for the pig.

It was used often in sacrifices to the gods by Kahuna priests. The animal was capable, too, of identifying evil sorcerers by its movements. And there were occasions when a high chief in exile had his identity revealed by a pig. The lowly animal had the intelligence to recognize nobility, and when he did, he always raised his snout.

THE SHARK MAN

Can a man change into an animal? That sounds ridiculous, but don't be too sure. In Hawaii, many strange things have happened, especially in the realm of sorcery. The story told by Walter J. Smith smacks of Huna magic.

According to Smith, there was once a man named Kawelo who lived on the left branch of the river near Lydgate Park. When he saw the canoes leaving the village, he would call out to the men, "Good morning. Where are you going?"

The reply would be, "We are going fishing."

Kawelo answered always, "The weather is good. I hope you have luck."

The fishermen would then paddle out to the ocean to fish. But on the day in question there was no fish. Instead, they were attacked by a huge shark. Some of the men were bitten and some were killed.

This was the state of affairs nearly every time they tried to catch fish. Kawelo would always wish them luck, and then they would be attacked by a shark.

One day the men decided to like to Kawelo. When he asked them where they were going, they replied that they were going to Holo-Holo (visit). Instead, they went fishing. They had good luck and there was no shark attack.

At a luau the men talked about Kawelo. Was he a god? Did he talk to sharks? Was he a sorcerer? The men didn't know, but they were suspicious. They decided that the next time they went fishing, they would send one man to spy on Kawelo.

So that was what they did. Kawelo waved to the men in the canoes and asked them where they were going. They replied that they were going fishing. The man who watched Kawelo saw him stand on a rock and wait for the canoes to sail out of sight. Then Kawelo dived into the water. The spy hurried closer to the water's edge. But Kawelo did not come to the surface. Instead, a huge shark came up and swam after the canoes.

The man was stunned. Nevertheless, he composed himself enough to run as quickly as he could toward the canoes at the mouth of the river. He waved his arms frantically and yelled. The men did not hear him.

He went back to the village and reported what had happened. The older men gathered everyone around them and announced that from then on no one would ever tell anyone that they were going fishing. It would be bad luck to do so. They were to say they were going Awana (wandering). Even today it is considered bad luck to tell anyone you are going fishing.

Did Kawelo have the ability to change from a man to a shark? You be the judge!

AKUA MO' O—THE LIZARD GOD

In 1795, Kamehameha the Great built a Hale Pua Niu in Waikiki. In this house, offerings were placed with the object of making a deceased person into an Akua Mo'o, a lizard god or goddess. Another object was to make the offerings for the existing Akua Mo'o.

The king built the house to keep his promise to an existing Akua Mo'o called Mo'o Kihawahine, a lizard goddess who had helped him conquer Oahu. He made the conquest in 1795 and built the Hale Pua Niu.

At one time, Mo'o Kihawahine was a real human, a high chieftess of Maui. Besides appearing as a lizard, the goddess took on the forms of a dog, a chicken or a spider. The Akua Mo'o was usually a giant lizard 12 to 30 feet in length. They could also make themselves as small as a skink (rock lizard) or a common house lizard. In the small size, they were known to listen in on the conversations of men. And there were a few Akua Mo'o who could assume the form of men.

Most Akua Mo'o live in fish ponds or at the base of a waterfall and still serve as guardians for Hawaiian families.

SHARK GUARDIAN

I have learned from certain people in Hawaii that quite a few of them still render obeisance to Kuula the shark god. They feel that their aumakuas are sharks. If you travel to the outer islands and walk along the isolated shores, you will hear from a cove the calling chant of fishermen who ask the shark for good fishing locations. The chant has been handed down from father to son for centuries. The guardian sharks still respond!

There are sharks perhaps 30 feet in length who have permitted five or six generations of children to ride their backs. The great animals also swam lazily beside the canoes and converse with the men while being fed tidbits.

One can still hear children of Vai Togi chant an old legend of a prince who was changed into a shark, and a princess who became a turtle. After a few minutes of chanting, you can look out toward the breaking surf and see the great creatures materialize!

KAHUNA ALOHA AND THE SHARK

Two elderly Hawaiians told me that on the Waianae Coast near Kaena Point there is a cove that is a lovers' lane, or more precisely a trysting place for lovers. Two young people not so long ago were very much in love but did not have family approval. They were watched constantly. They could never be alone.

Desperate, the young man went to see a Kahuna Aloha, who is a priest for lovers. The wise man promised to help him in return for a basket of eggs. The eggs were supplied, and the Kahuna turned the young man into a shark so that he could swim through an underground tunnel that led into the cove. There, the wahine waited every night unobserved.

I was told that if I had the courage to crawl through that dangerous inner cove, I would hear the lover's voices. I decided to take their word for it.

THE HEALING SHARK

Another ancient Hawaiian, a woman, told me that when she was young she had a grandfather who was always sick. Whenever he felt particularly low, he would tell the little girl to go to a special spot near the shore and feed the white shark that was there. She did. And every time she returned home, her grandfather felt better.

Chapter 10:
Kahuna Herbal Remedies For A Better You!

Timothy Green Beckley

Kahuna Herbal Remedies For A Better You!

One thing you notice right away about the native Hawaiians is that they all look exceedingly healthy. It's obvious that they eat right, sleep well, and above all else, know how to relax in an often all too complex world.

Today, holistic medicine has become very popular as more and more people realize that prescription drugs are not the sole cure-all to our many ailments. Indeed, herbs, roots and other homeopathic remedies have existed in many cultures and have been utilized for centuries, long before doctors were licensed to practice by the American Medical Association.

The Kahuna had at their disposal all sorts of natural remedies. In Hawaii, many herbs exist that are believed to be powerful natural medicines, and, to this day, there are some on the Islands who would rather depend on nature than go to visit a physician.

Of course, we live in a modern world and fully realize the great advances made by the medical profession in many areas. Today, it is possible to stay well and look healthy way up in years. And, in addition, it is true that many diseases have been eliminated in our lifetime. But, perhaps we should not discount totally the folklore remedies that appear to have helped so many "primitive" peoples for so long. Perhaps a combination of both modern and herbal medicines would be of added benefit to giving us an even healthier world. Maybe—just maybe—we should listen to what the Kahuna have to say regarding this important subject.

--Maria H. Carta

◀ ▼ ▶

Kahuna Power

We had absolutely no way of knowing when we first eyed the elderly man sitting in the middle of Plantation Hale's modern shopping center weaving a papalo (hat), that this same charming gentleman would prove to be so beneficial in our quest to crack the secret society of the Kahuna. Looking back to the day we arrived on the Island of Kauai, I would bet, however, that it was more than mere "coincidence" that we both stopped and took notice as Joseph Iida went about his meticulous task, which he does a couple of times a week, for the benefit of tourists who are interested in seeing how things were once woven by hand before the invention of the sewing machine.

Following the front-page story about us that appeared in THE GARDEN ISLANDER, the telephone in our hotel suite rang several times. The callers all appeared eager to share a bit of Kahuna knowledge with us, since they could somehow "sense" our sincerity in spreading the word back to the mainland about this all-so-wise magically oriented culture.

Of all those who called (or approached us on the street), the eighty-year-old weaver would end up sharing a great deal of knowledge about the subjects of herbal remedies and his personal experiences with the enigmatic goddess of the Fiftieth State, Madame Pele.

Unlike most Hawaiians, who would consider it betraying a confidence if they reveal too much about the "practices" of the Kahuna to outsiders, Joseph doesn't feel the same way because he is not really Hawaiian, but is of mixed ancestry. "My father was Japanese, my mother Portuguese," he explains. "My grandparents were among the first Orientals to come here. Around 1885, my grandmother had a beautiful baby girl who the Queen took a liking to because she was so pretty. The Queen asked my grandmother if she could take the child, which was considered to be a great honor. My grandmother said 'No!' even though it would mean she would have been richly rewarded. The Queen said that if she didn't give her the baby, the child would never make it off the Islands. As it turned out, she died at a young age, before she could visit the Orient." Joseph is not sure if this was the result of a Kahuna curse or just an unfortunate coincidence.

Iida's grandparents and parents were among the few outsiders to learn all about the Huna faith, and Joseph keeps the traditions alive as he discusses them with those who he feels may benefit the most from these mystical practices.

Though his father kept a black book with all the herbal remedies written down in it, the book mysteriously vanished when Joe's dad passed away. But despite his advanced years, Mr. Iida has absolutely no trouble with his memory, and thus has been able to preserve all the knowledge of the Kahuna priests that has been passed down to him.

"My father had bleeding ulcers and, when he went to the hospital, they said that he would have to have an operation," the soft spoken resident of Lihue said as he began telling us how the herbal remedies of the Islands had always worked for those he loved. "Instead of going for a treatment, he took a certain mixture composed of a type of soil taken from near the beach and dabbled it on the infected area. He was well in no time and never had to see a doctor again for this problem." Joseph says he personally remembers seeing an Hawaiian man break his leg in three places and, when they treated his wound with a packing made up of the same mixture, the man was able to get up and go about his business in only a week.

One of the concoctions Joseph sings the praises of is made from an herb known on Kauai as *Mamakie*. "This plant makes an excellent herbal tea that will bring a person's blood pressure right down. I've also used it to help individuals with sugar diabetes eat whatever they want, as the tea acts as a neutralizer in their system." Joseph suggests drinking one cup of the tea with each meal, and says, "It tastes really good when mixed with honey or lemon."

Joseph Iida stayed with us for the better part of an entire day, and we have corresponded since returning home. Though he could not share all his knowledge in the limited time allowed for us to be together, he did talk at length about his encounters with the spirit of Madame Pele, which we delve into in detail in the final chapter of this book.

AUTHOR'S WARNING

IT IS EXTREMELY IMPERATIVE THAT ALL READERS REFRAIN FROM TESTING ANY AND ALL OF THE HERBAL REMEDIES DESCRIBED IN THIS BOOK WITHOUT CONSULTING A QUALIFIED PHYSICIAN AND OBTAINING HIS OR HER APPROVAL. YOUR PARTICULAR PHYSICAL CONDITION MAY NOT BE COMPATIBLE WITH WHAT IS RECOMMENDED IN THESE PAGES.

The remedies in this section have been taken from sources thought to be authenticated, but should be treated only as regional folklore. None of these herbal remedies, to our knowledge, have ever been properly tested under scientific conditions, although we have heard of increased interest by members of the medical profession in some of these supposed "cure-alls."

THE SELECTING OF HERBS

The Kahuna gathers his herbs early in the morning to avoid being disturbed by distracting noises or actions. When he finds the plant he is looking for, he prays to Ku and Hina, and then to the god of the plant he is collecting.

The prayer below is invoked for someone who has trouble with his eyes. The Kahuna says his prayer to Kane-I-ka-popolo after he has found a large popolo plant standing alone.

I hele mai nei au e noi ia oe, e Kane-I-ka-popolo
I have come here to request you, o Kane-I-ka-popolo

I la'au e oia ai ku'u maka (a I 'ole o mea)
Medicine that (name) eyes may be healed

I ulu iluna
That grew above

I lala iluna
That stood above

I liko iluna
That branched above

I 'opu iluna
That opened its flowers above

I mohala iluna
That full bloomed above

I pua iluna
That flowered above

I hua a 'o'o iluna
That bore fruit and matured above

I pala iluna
That ripened above.

For other ailments, the Kahuna changes the second line to read, *"Medicine that (name) (other ailments) may be healed."* After the prayer is spoken, the Kahuna picks one leaf on the right side of the plant, one on the left side, and one in the middle of the plant. That is his pattern, and he continues in that manner until he has the number of leaves he needs. His prayer now is: **O ke ola o ka la'au, a Kane, no ku'u maka. 'Amama.** *"Grant the healing power of your medicine, O Kane, for my eyes. It is finished. I have been healed."*

The Kahuna then pounds five leaves until they are soft. He mixes them with the Water-of-Kane and squeezes them through white tapa cloth. The juice is applied to the eyes for five days.

While selecting his plants, the Kahuna may also pray:

Listen, Ku

I have come to gather (plant) for (patient's name)
This (plant) which was rooted in Kahiki
Spread its rootlets in Kahiki
Produced stalk in Kahiki
Budded in Kahiki
Bore fruit in Kahiki
Life is from you, O Ku
Until he/she crawls feebly and totters in extreme old age
Until the blossoming at the end.

'AWA

This is similar to a tranquilizer. It makes one relax and go to sleep. People with fevers take 'awa because it is important to sleep when the body temperature is high. It was also used as a tonic to combat weakness. The 'awa was prepared by drying the root in the sun, then chopping it into small pieces. It was then chewed. One and a half quarts of water were mixed with five mouthfuls and strained through fibers of makaloa. The liquid was then heated with in a calabash with water and red-hot stones. The patient waited for the mixture to cool, then drank it until he fell asleep.

Mothers bothered with restless children would chew the leaf bud, then give it to their children to chew mornings and evenings.

Men who worked hard all day often made the mixture with coconut milk. Their sore muscles eased. 'Awa was also used when one could not pass urine, or had a bad headache, or lung troubles, or when a woman's womb was displaced.

WILD GINGER

This herb has large, knobby underground stems. When cut, they give off a spicy aroma. The stems were washed and ground in a stone mortar with a stone pestle. Water was added, then strained through fibers of makaloa, which is a Hawaiian sedge. The clear liquid was then consumed to cure a stomachache.

Expert on Kahuna practices and Hawaiian folklore, Joseph Iida holds several containers filled with herbal remedies. (photo by Tim Beckley)

PANDANUS OR SCREWPINE

The tips of the aerial roots were pulled off, and the root tip was pounded with other plants and the juice of sugar cane. The juice was squeezed and strained, then heated by dropping hot stones into the mixture.

Mothers who were weak from bearing too many children drank this for strength. So did anyone who suffered pains in the chest. It was also used as a laxative for children and adults.

HAU

In the bark of its branches and in the flower there is a slimy sap that is used as medicine. It was used as a mild laxative for children. Before children grow teeth, mothers would chew the bud and then give it to the children to swallow. Buds were also chewed and swallowed for dry throat. The bark of the stem was used for congested chests and mothers in labor.

INDIGO

This plant was brought to Hawaii about 150 years ago for the purpose of making a blue dye. However, the process proved too costly and since then the plant has grown wild.

Indigo is used for backaches, rheumatism and for womb problems. The whole plant was pounded with other plants and salt. When mixed with water, the medicine was used for a hard, dry cough.

TI

Hawaiians plant ti around their houses to bring them good luck. It was also used for growths in the nose. The ti flowers were pounded with other plants and ginger roots. The juice was squeezed and strained. Little balls of tree-fern hairs (pulu) were made and then soaked in the liquid. The patient breathed the vapor given off in the tree-fern ball five or six times a day. Ti flowers with other plants were used as an elixir for asthma. Ti leaves were dipped in cold spring water and placed on the forehead of one who suffered with a headache or fever. Hot stones wrapped in ti leaves were used for sore backs.

KOA

Bedridden patients sometimes needed something soft to lie on. The leaves of the Koa tree were used to make the patient more comfortable. The patient would sweat because of the leaves, and thereby break his fever.

GUAVA

The use here was for deep cuts, sprains and other injuries. The leaf buds were pounded with other plants and the juice was squeezed directly on the injured part. It was also used for diarrhea.

CANDLENUT

The kernel of this plant was used in bad cases of constipation. The meat of the ripe nut was pounded, mixed with other plants, and applied to skin sores and ulcerated skin. The same plant with other plants, mixed, was a tonic to build up one's body. Babies with mouth sores ('ea) were given this remedy after the mother chewed the flowers, spread the sap on her fingers and then applied it to the sores on the baby's mouth and tongue.

COMMON PLANTAIN

This is a weed and was used as a tonic, as a cure for constipation and for boils. Adults chewed four or five leaves and swallowed them to achieve regular bowel movements. To get rid of a boil, two leaves were rubbed together with some salt until they were soft. The entire boil was then covered with the leaves. A narrow piece of tapa cloth was made into a ring and applied to the eye of the boil and tied with a bandage also made from tapa cloth. Every morning, a fresh application was put on the boil until it broke and the core came out.

SEAWEED

Two types of seaweed and baked taro were chewed by a mother with a weak baby. She would give it to the child twice a day until the age of six months. For a person who was recovering slowly from a sickness, a lei of seaweed was made for him. He wore the lei as he walked slowly into the ocean. The lei were not tied in those days. They were open. As the patient walked against the waves, the water would take the lei, and with it the remaining sickness.

BANANA

When a person was weak and had a coated tongue from stomach trouble, he took the sap from the cut flower bud, pounded it and drank the juice. The mixture was used for stomach cramps. The liquid was taken for constipation and to build up weak babies. The banana, as we know, is rich in vitamins.

POLYNESIAN ARROWROOT

Hawaiians grated the tubers and put the material in a calabash with water. The starch settled on the bottom. Every day for several days the water was poured off and fresh water added. This was done to get rid of the bitterness of the pia starch. The starch was then spread on a flat stone to dry. It was then ground up into a powder and was taken as a cure for diarrhea and dysentery.

PRICKLY POPPY OR BEACH POPPY

Hawaiians call this plant Pua-kala. It is thorny like the kala fish. The plant has a yellow sap which was used to cure toothaches, neuralgia and ulcers.

SWEET POTATO

This was used to induce vomiting when one ate something bad, or too much. The meat of the tuber was scraped and placed in water, along with ti-stem meat, and then placed in the sun to warm up. After straining, it was taken internally. The tubers from other varieties of sweet potatoes helped to cure asthma, sleeplessness, and troubles of the womb. The leaves were mixed with other plants to use as a laxative for children and to give them strength. Mothers who could not produce enough milk for their babies wore a lei of sweet potato vine around their neck. The vine had a milky sap which was supposed to make her milk flow.

WALTHERIA

The bark of mature roots was chewed, and the juice swallowed, for three or four days to cure a sore throat. As a treatment for asthma, the roots, leaves, buds and flowers were pounded together. The juice was pressed out and the liquid strained. Every morning the juice was heated. After five days, the asthma was gone.

BREADFRUIT

If parts of the tree are broken off, a sticky, milky sap flows. It is used for skin diseases, cuts, scratches, and scaly and cracked skin. Sores around the mouth are treated with the sap as well.

HERBAL TREATMENTS

Before treating the patient, the Kahuna is likely to address the four great gods: Ku, Kane, Kanaloa and Lono. With his arms outstretched, he will call to the god of healing, not only for help in curing the patient, but to assure himself of the right method. Although he knows how to treat his patient, he wants a nod from the gods to make sure he is right. He may pray for hours.

At such times, this is the prayer of the Kahuna:

I Hiiaka paha oe, I Hiialo, I kakahiaka nei
Perhaps thou are in Hiiaka, perhaps in Hiialo, this morning

I ka laaua a (inoa) medicine
Give virtue to (name) medicine

A hiki is Maul-ola I ka heiau I Mahina-uli
Grant him great vigor, and let him attain health

I ola is Mauli-ola
To worship at the heiau of Mahina-uli.

ANEMIA

The herb is 'alaea, which is used when a patient has a wound or is bleeding internally. The herb is crushed to a powder and a pinch of it is added to food. It mixes easily with pi, sweet potato, yams and breadfruit. The pinch should be large.

ASTHMA

The white flower of the pua-kala is used for asthma, but only if the flower stands up straight. If it leans to the uplands, it is not to be used. It is pounded soft, mixed with water, strained and then drunk. Prayer should always accompany treatment. The phlegm will come up.

BLOAT

The remedy is many greens with meals. The best are the leaves of the popolo and the young leaves of the sweet potato. Increase the intake of limu (seaweed).

BRONCHITIS

The treatment is mau'u kukae pua'a, the bright yellow base of hala key, which is used to make a lei. Combine it with raw kukui nuts.

CANCER

Divide into five equal parts the stem of the flower of a bunch of bananas of the Iholena variety. Each piece is used for each treatment, morning and night until the five pieces are gone. Pound each piece with two segments of sugarcane (elua puna ko) until thoroughly mashed. Strain well and drink the juice. Also, pound the tip of the aerial root of the hala. Squeeze out the juice and drink five times a day.

CIRCULATION

Boiled limu (seaweed) is the prescription. The hot water, which contains iodine, should be applied.

COLDS, TONSILLITIS, COUGHS

If a cold results in a rundown condition, slowly boil the bark of the mountain apple tree. Drink some before each meal. Also, cook young popolo leaves in a calabash with hot stones. Squeeze the juice and drink it. To cure a cough, eat the young popolo leaves either raw or cooked. For a sore throat, gargle with the sap from a raw sweet potato mixed with a small amount of water. For chills, chop awa into small bits, enough to fill four cups. Pound in an equal amount of water. Take four cups of 'ohi'a-ai buds and leaves, add one green kukui nut, and twenty ko'oko'o lau buds and flowers. Pound the mix thoroughly and strain. Cook with heated stones and take three times a day with meals for five days.

CONSTIPATION

The roots of the pohuehue, pounded and then eaten. Also, the fruit of the 'akala, eaten in great quantities, is effective. Another good laxative is made by boiling the whole moa plant. Should a strong purge be needed, eat the seeds of the kakalaioa. Another strong remedy is the flowers of the hau, 'ilima, and noni. The male hau is the Hau koi'I—it has the power. The leaf is pointed.

CONSUMPTION

One potion is formed by taking four ripe fruits of the noni, one bunch of 'ihi'awa in the amount you can take in encircling the thumb and forefinger. The flower should be pink; the white flower is for children. Pound all of it soft and place in a clean poi-straining cloth. Do not pound with water. Wring it dry and place it in a bowl used for eating poi. Turn the front of the body downward, place a pillow under the chest so that part of the body is high. The patient should then drink the medicine. Administer between four and six in the afternoon. The patient should lie still for thirty minutes. You can tell when the medicine is taking effect when the patient suffers nausea, confusion and sluggishness. Five potions should be administered in five days. On the last day, an 'a'ama crab should be eaten along with other foods like poi, taro, or a sweet potato. The crab can be eaten raw or cooked, but its legs should not be broken.

DEBILITY

The leaves and flowers of the ko'oko'olau, dried and made into a tea, or the leaves of the popolo, which can be eaten green or cooked. Chewing the bark of the 'akoko is effective.

DIABETES

The traditional medicine still in use in Hawaii is the kolomona. The bark is stripped and dried, then boiled in water until the liquid looks like black tea. It should be taken three times a day after meals. It is important that one drinks no more than three cups a day. Caution is suggested here. One patient brought her blood sugar level down to 54 and went into a coma. The scraped bark from the kolomona should be yellow. If it's orange, don't use it. Also, the hinahina that grows along the beach is good. Use it as a tea.

EARACHE

Pound 'olena, put it into a cloth, warm it, then squeeze it. Let the drops all into the ear.

GOUT

The leaves, buds and flowers of the ko'oko'olau should be pounded thoroughly. Drink the juice. A tea can be made from the leaves. Take five times a day until cured. Another cure is the juice from the fully ripened noni fruit.

HEMORROIDS

Pluck a handful of uhaloa flowers and eat them.

HIGH BLOOD PRESSURE

Mash ripe noni, drink the juice while eating. Take it for five days and repeat until cured.

INSECT STING

Cut the stem of any kind of taro and rub it on the afflicted area.

JAUNDICE

'Apu kowali was the medicine used in 1870 by a Kahuna. After taking the medicine, the patient excreted. The Kahuna bathed him in hot water and administered an enema purge. The treatment lasted for four weeks and the patient was cured.

KIDNEY AND BLADDER DISORDERS

With the right hand, gather five noni blossoms and five fruits, then pray to Ku. Eat the fruit and the blossoms. Next, use the left hand and five blossoms and five fruit. Pray to Hina. Then eat the fruit and blossoms. Repeat for five days, alternating hands. Another remedy is to consume the seeds of the nohu.

MENSTRUAL DISORDER

Look in the sandy area along beaches for the hinahina. It has small white flowers and small green hairy leaves. Boil it in salt water. The liquid is dark in color. Taken for three days in the morning and evening before meals. It will also clear away blood clots.

PILES

One piece of 'olena root, pound until soft. Add 'alaea and mix with water. Rub it on the tender area.

RHEUMATISM

Boil large quantities of wawae-'iole moss, let it cool, then bathe the patient. Drink a cup of 'awa twice a day. Also, fry Hawaiian salt, place in a bag, and apply to painful areas two or three times a day or night.

SINUS DISORDERS

Pound 'olena until soft, bake it, and insert carefully into the nose with a grass stem.

STIFFNESS

When joints are stiff, bind four or five kukui leaves to the joint overnight. Repeat as often as necessary.

TOOTHACHE

Look for the root of the puakala, cut a plug and insert into cavity. The tooth allegedly will never cause you trouble again.

TUBERCULOSIS

Take five fruits of the noni, pound. Gather five segments of either the sugarcane 'ele'ele or maikoiko, and pound. Take enough 'awa to fill two hands, pound. Mix all three ingredients and add 'alaea. Cook in a calabash. Take five times a day until cured.

URINARY DISORDERS

This medicine is for painful urination. It is kukui. Take 32 kukui nuts, crack them, shell them, get the meat. Chew it until it's soft, then place in a bowl, then put in water. Rub them about in the water. Strain and clean them. Drink the medicine, then sit down. If the urine comes out and there is no pain, the patient is cured.

REMEDIES EXTOLLED BY THE KAHUNA

It must be pointed out here as a reminder that none of these cures should be attempted without the permission of your physician. Your doctor must be consulted at all times.

BACKACHE

A Kahuna friend told me that the way he treated a backache was to take the entire puakola plant and a handful of iniko leaves and a teaspoon of Hawaiian salt and pound them or grind them together. The resultant mash is then placed in the center of a folded cloth or towel. Roll the towel lengthwise. Hold the towel over a large bowl and twist the ends of the towel so that the juice from the mash drips into the bowl. To each tablespoon of juice add one cup of water. Drink a small glassful of this concoction each morning for five days. If the taste is disagreeable, chew a piece of coconut. Drink no alcoholic beverages or coffee during the treatment period. Weak tea is all right.

The backache, if severe, can be treated with a poultice of crushed koali root, pounded with salt. The poultice should applied to the afflicted area for one half hour while the patient is awake.

According to the Kahuna, there are people who find relief from a backache by drinking cold tea made from the ripe noni fruit. Squeeze the juice out through a cloth. Add a glass of water to one tablespoon of juice and drink several times a day.

Other patients prefer a warm tea made from lapine leaves. It has a citrus taste and smells of ginger. Take two or three dried leaves and wrinkle them between the hands. Drop them into boiling water. Drink the tea every morning.

BLISTERS

Blisters on the hands or feet can be treated with a poultice of popolo leaves, pounded with a tablespoon of Hawaiian salt to make a paste. Cover the blister with the poultice and tie it in place.

CHAPPED LIPS

If applied in time, a small drop of hinu hino will stop the spread of chapped lips. To prevent the condition, use your forefinger to collect the oil from the side of your nose and rub it on the lips. If the chapping is serious, use the sap from kukui twigs.

CHARLEY HORSE

For any kind of cramp in the leg or arm, it is a good idea to keep a rounded stone on hand. An iron ball is good, too. Heat the stone or ball (not too hot) and roll it over the sore area. Or make a poultice of koali root, ground with salt. Bind it into place over the sore spot.

COLD HANDS

Cool weather can make a woman's hands rather unsightly. The fingertips become white and the skin blotchy. You may find some response with the use of pohe kula. You will need about a quart of the leaves. Pound them with the bark of a taproot and a tablespoon of Hawaiian salt. Strain mixture through a cloth. Drink a teaspoon of the juice mixed with a glass of water every day until the condition is gone. You can also eat a few of the leaves every day in a salad after the condition has cleared up.

GARGLE

When you need to gargle there are two concoctions that are good. One is a tablespoon of Hawaiian salt in a pint of fresh water. The other is using the kukui trees if they are in bloom. Gather a quart of blossoms with a piece of kukui bark about the size of the hand. Also the same size of ohia-lehua bark. Grind them all together with a tablespoon of salt, strain and add to milk from a coconut. Refrigerate.

HEARTBURN

Select four young shoots of pakikawaio and grind them with a quart of fresh iliohe. Add two tablespoons of Hawaiian salt, and then add a dozen thoroughly cooked young taro leaves. This will be your only food for one day. You may have tea made with ko (oko'olau). Follow up the next day with a mild laxative and eat sparingly. No tobacco or alcohol should be taken during the treatment.

IMPOTENCY

Strip the bark from four olapa roots and pound them with the same amount of pipi and two joints of ko. Add one quart of fresh water, mix and strain through a cloth. Drink one-half cup of fluid every morning and evening until the mixture is gone. Take no alcohol and do not smoke during the treatment.

INDIGESTION

Make a tea of awapuhi pake. The amount to use is about the size of two joints of a finger. Use a quart of water. Bring to a boil, and then simmer for a few minutes. Drink a cupful before each meal until you have relief.

INFECTION

Try to open the wound to let it drain. Take a piece of the inner bark of koa (about the size of your hand) with two tablespoons of Hawaiian salt. Pound. Allow the koa juice to drip into the wound, then place the fiber against the infection and bind with cloth. Repeat the treatment morning and evening, but leave the wound open to the sun in the afternoon. Sometimes an infection responds to taro leaves. Mash six taro leaves with a handful of Hawaiian salt. Apply this poultice to the infection and cover it with a large taro leaf. Change the poultice three times a day until the infection is gone.

INHALER

To make an inhaler that will clear the head, correct shortness of breath and improve one's disposition, mash a pint of the tender tips of a'ali'l with ten flowers of awa-puhi keokeo. Add a tablespoon of juice from a joint of ko. Add a ball of pulu about the size of a man's thumb and mix these ingredients well. Allow it to dry in the sun, then roll it into small sticks no larger than one's little finger. When they are dry enough to hold together, insert gently into the nostrils.

INSOMNIA

Gather the sticky tips of the a'ali'l bush. Dry slowly in hot shade. You may then store in an airtight container and use it as tobacco. Two or three pipefuls should cause drowsiness. Awa as described earlier assures one of many hours of sleep without any drowsiness when awakened. When a lack of sleep brings one to the border of insanity, it is recommended that ipu awaawa be used. The patient eats the young shoots and the leaves. Then he chews a piece of dried coconut with sweet potato twice a day for five days. Then the patient rests for a full day. He then eats the meat from two fully matured fruits. That is followed by an internal bath (enema) and an external bath.

NERVOUSNESS

Awa is good for a nervous condition, but one has to be careful not to overindulge. There are side effects. The skin may scale and peel as with sunburn. Lomi (massage) is also good if performed by a Kahuna master of massage. If one is not available, then a rubdown is helpful.

NEURALGIA

Select four uhaloa roots and two handfuls of awa. Grind together. Place in a pan with six cups of water and bring to a boil. Let it simmer for ten to fifteen minutes. Cover. Cool, then strain through a cloth. This tea should be taken one half cup at a time, twice a day for five days. If you don't like the taste, eat a banana or a piece of dried coconut. After the treatment is finished, take a mild laxative.

RASH

This condition is treated externally and internally at the same time. For the bath, collect about 40 auhuhu leaves, four pieces of puakala root bark, a quart of a'ali'l leaves and a teaspoon of Hawaiian salt. Pound all together through a cloth and it to a gallon of fresh water. Bring the solution to a boil, cover it and let it simmer on a low flame for about 30 minutes. When the concoction is cool enough, sponge the body with the solution. Repeat several times a day until the rash and itching go away. A glass of awa is made by taking small pieces of the root and chewing them. When you have three cuds of awa, about the size of one's thumb, place them in a bowl and mash them with a cup of water. Strain through a cloth, remove the woody material and drink the juice.

HERBAL MEDICINES FOR CHILDREN

At the time of weaning, the Kahuna haha pa'ao'ao spoke the following prayer:

E lono, e Kane, e Nua-kea, ka wahine isia ka poli-waiu o ke keiki
O Lono, O Kane, O Nua-kea, the woman with breastful of milk for child

Eia ke ukuki nei o Mea
We are about to wean (name)

E lawe aku oe I ka waiu o ka makuahine
Staunch the flow of milk in his mother

Ia oe e ka la, ka mahine, ka hoku
Yours are the sun, the moon and the stars

E lawe oe e kukulu o Kahiki
Carry away to the pillars of Kahiki

Haalele aku I ka omimo, ka uwe wale o Mea
And there leave the emaciation, peevishness and wailing of the child

A e hanai oe I ka la kapu a Kane
Feed him with the sacred fish of Kane

Oia ka hilu
That is reposed and quiet

Ka noho malie, Kane
This is your blessing, O Kane

Amama. Ua noa.
Amen. The prayer is ended.

Actually, the Kahuna haha pa'ao'ao, who in modern times would be called a pediatrician, began his treatment of the baby a few days after it was born. Before that there were months of prayers and offerings to all of the gods, greater and lesser, strict observance of the kapu, and selected foods and herbs for the mother-to-be.

When the baby came, he was patted on the back to remove the mucous from his nose. If any remained inside, the grandparents would suck it out after first rinsing their mouths. Birth fluids were disgorged by putting a finger down into the baby's throat.

A sharp bamboo knife was used to cut the umbilical cord. A kupa was wound around the child's waist and he was not bathed until the cord fell off. The cord had to be disposed of in the right way, because an improper method could affect the baby's personality. If a rat ate it, for instance, the child would grow up to be a thief. If the cord was thrown into the sea, the child would develop a love of water.

The baby's eyes were pressed inward at the corners with a thumb and forefinger. The head was molded and the ears were pressed flat. The fingers were gently rolled. The male child had his buttocks flattened. The girl's mons veneris was rubbed with kukui nut oil to make it beautifully rounded. These moldings and proddings continued until the child was grown.

If the mother's milk did not appear right away, pounded sweet potato was plastered to the anterior fontanel (soft spot) so that the baby was fed by absorption. When the mother's milk came, the fontanel was plastered with popolo. This drew out a hidden disease known as 'ea huna, which was present in every child. The treatment also helped to close the fontanel.

The mother's milk supply was stimulated with the help of ko'oko'olau, ilima blossoms and the base of the hua blossoms. A ritual toward this end was for the mother to pick one sweet potato with her right hand while praying to Ku, and one with her left hand while praying to Hina.

In still another ritual, the mother rose at dawn to fill a bowl with wai puna (fresh spring water). She placed the sweet potato vines she picked the day before into the water. She took the vine she picked with the right hand and struck her breast while praying to Ku for a good supply of milk. She next took the vine she picked with her left hand and struck her breast while praying to Hina.

Her prayer for abundant milk was: "La ola a Ku a me Hina. Homai ka waiu a nui a lawa a helehele'I ola ka olua a haawi mai ai ka olua pulapula." "That life, O Ku and Hina, extend the milk till there is much and sufficient and scattered about. That is for you to give your offspring and for the land to multiply."

If the mother still did not lactate, the tender leaves of the noni were heated and placed on the mother's breast while more prayers were invoked to Ku and Hina. Herbs like moa and the greens of the sweet potato were given to her so that the baby would benefit from them through the milk.

On the fifth day after birth, the Kahuna examined the baby for pa'ao'ao and 'ea. These are two diseases not easily defined in medical terms in use today. Apparently, they caused fretfulness, whining, stomach upsets and a sickly appearance. To this layman, I would think of colic.

The herbs used to treat pa'ao'ao were ko'oko'olau and makou. Other herbs were the flowers and the bark of the kokoi, the flowers of the 'ilima and uhaloa, the left and taproot of the hinahina and the aerial root of the hala. The baby, of course, could not eat these herbs. He was given them through his mother's milk. Later, she would chew the herbs and then place them in the baby's mouth.

To treat 'ea, the baby was given thoroughly chewed kauna 'oa pehu, or the 'ilima blossoms, especially those that grew near the shore, popolo blossoms, the blossoms of hibiscus or the root of the hinihina kahaki.

At the age of ten months, the child was tested to determine whether he was ready for weaning. The Kahuna made the test. The mother held the child so that it faced him. The Kahuna placed two stones in front of the child. If he threw one away, he was ready for weaning. If not, the test was given again in a few weeks.

DEFORMED CHILDREN

It was wrongly believed that all deformed children in Hawaii were disposed of. Captain James King, who sailed with Captain Cook, wrote: "We saw here more deformed people than in all other islands put together. Some had prominances before and behind, or were what we call humped back. One young man had neither feet nor hands. We saw two dwarfs. One was an old man four feet, two inches, perfectly well made. The other was a fat, chubby woman, and many of their lower class people were ill made. They brought to us a blind man to be cured, and a squinting sight was pretty common."

The skeletons of adults found (buried before Cook's arrival in the Islands) proved that the deformed were never disposed of. The deformities ranged from clubfeet to spinal abnormalities.

The Kahuna doctors treated these people with Iomilomi (massage and manipulation). Sea bathing was another treatment, as was sweet potato packs, soft poi applications, and in the case of a weak child, partial burial in the sand. Mother's milk in the eyes helped those with weak vision. If a baby's eyes were weak, the Kahuna blew a chewed leaf of a lele banana across the eyes. A child who had fits was given salt and ashes. A deaf child was treated with the juice of pua kala, and a child who lost his voice was given wauke malolo to eat.

Chapter 11:
Ritualistic Burials— A Descent Into Hell

Ritualistic Burials – A Descent Into Hell

The burial rites of others living in far off lands may sometimes seem strange those who reside in large, modern countries. But are our burial rites any more "civilized" in structure when you come to think about the whole idea of death and dying? After all, isn't it peculiar that we lay our loved ones, who we are in the midst of mourning, inside an elongated box known as a coffin, to eventually place them a good six feet down in the ground?

Why, then, should we think others, such as the Kahuna, should be considered odd for doing things their own individual way?

To the Kahuna, death was of uppermost importance, and it truly mattered how a body was disposed of. In fact, the way in which an individual was laid to rest indicated what social position that person held in life. If a person had died due to sorcery, the Kahuna sought instant revenge. In some respects, the ways in which the Hawaiians were buried are somewhat similar to burial customs of other cultures, in particular the Orientals and the Native-Americans. The Chinese often have a small parade carry the casket through the streets while holding up a photo of the person who rests inside. In many ways, such funerals were a celebrations, as the Kahuna offered food and drink as part of the ceremonies.

Many today might see the Kahuna burial rites as a descent into the lower regions of hell. The crude coffins look truly weird, and the various ways in which they tried to absorb the pain of the grieving is certainly worth reading about in our quest to understand other cultures besides our own.

--Maria H. Carta

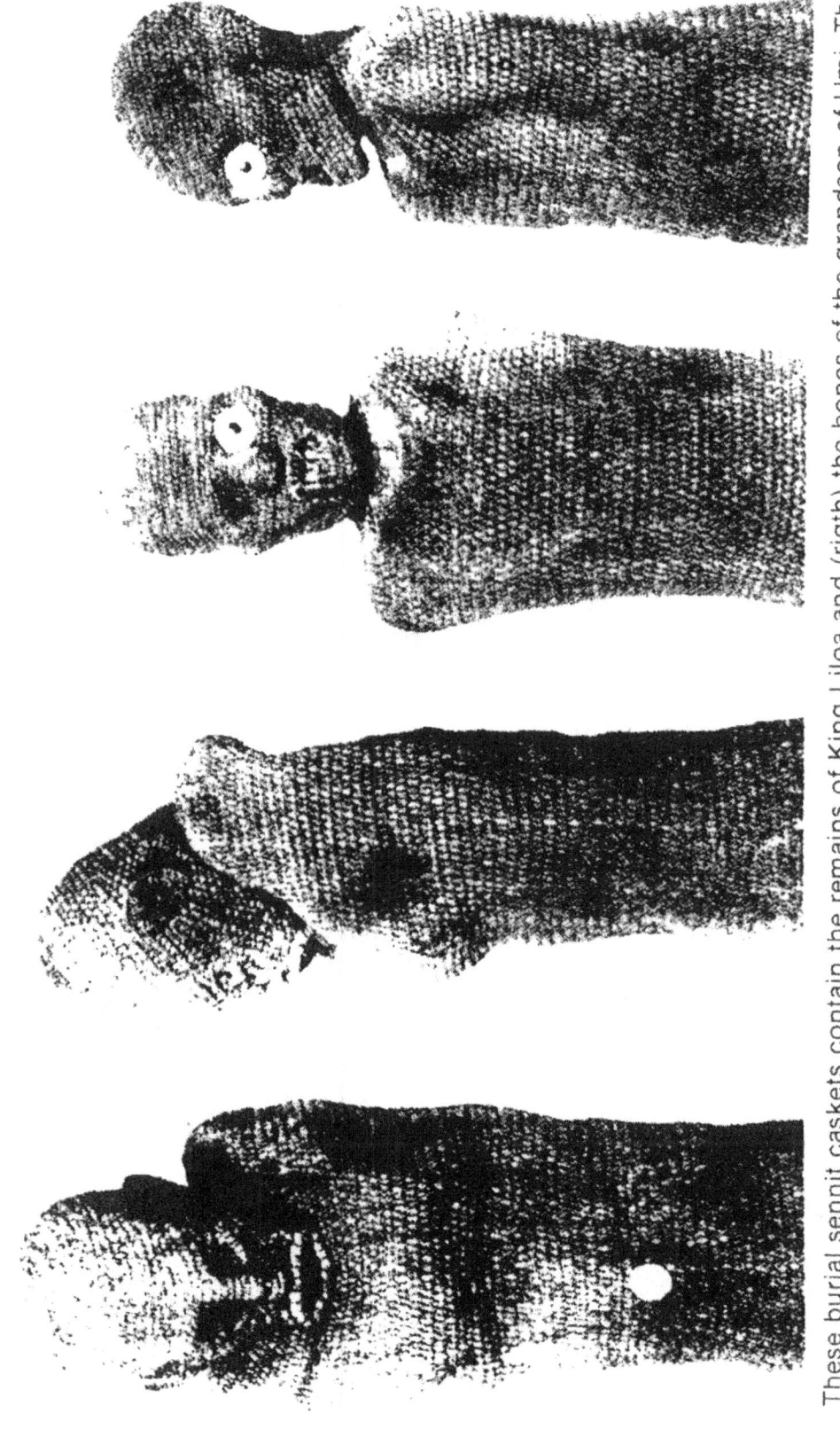

These burial sennit caskets contain the remains of King Liloa and (rigth) the bones of the grandson of Umi. The caskets are now in the custody of the Bishop Museum.

I listened to a group of Hawaiians talk of the days long ago when the burial of a Hawaiian meant excruciating pain for the living. They told me that when a chief died, a period of kapu lasted for 10 days or more. If a commoner died, the period was only two days. The kapu applied to the house that held the deceased and to the relatives. The food, too, was under kapu. Anyone who came into contact with the grieving relatives, or touched their food, was defiled. He was infectious to others until a priest removed the kapu with a ceremony.

Neighbors marched to the house of death weeping and wailing in the belief that a free flow of tears helps to soothe the agony of grief. Friends and relatives of the deceased cut their hair and disfigured their bodies.

A mourner would have an incisor knocked out with a stick and a stone. Some had a tooth knocked out for each death, until eventually all of their incisors were gone.

On rare occasions, a mourner would cut off one or both of his ears. More common was the practice of tattooing a black spot or line on the tongue. It was said that Queen Kamamalu, wife of Liholiho, was having a line tattooed on her tongue when she raised her hands to stop the tattoo artist for a while. He asked her about the pain. She said, "The pain is indeed great, but the pain of my grief is greater."

Burning of the skin was also a mark of mourning. A strip of bark was removed from a small branch about one inch in diameter. The bark was worked into a tube. One end was lighted and applied to the face or the breast. A blister formed. Later, there would be a permanent scar.

The body itself was wrapped in tapa, either in the extended or flexed position. If the body was dissected, then the bones (some of them) were wrapped in tapa. An extended body was easy to wrap. A flexed body required that the corpse be manipulated. A rope was attached to the joints of the legs and then passed around the neck. The rope was dawn tight until the knees touched the chest. This put the body into a round shape and it was then wrapped tightly in tapa.

Chief's bodies were sometimes salted. A transverse incision was made, across the upper abdomen below the ribs, and the insides were removed. The cavity was then filled with salt. The body was called an I'a loa (long fish) and was undoubtedly kept a long time before burial.

DEATH BY SORCERY

If it was determined that a person had died because of sorcery, a Kahuna kuni was hired to bring about the death of the sorcerer through a kuni ceremony. The dead person's liver was removed and cut up into small pieces. Those pieces were stuffed into the bodies of dogs and fowl, and the dead animals were burned to ashes in a fire ritual. When the ceremony was finished, the person's body was buried.

SAND BURIALS

In 1937, at Mokapu, Oahu, bulldozers leveled some sand dunes so that houses could be constructed on the site. More than 300 perfect skeletons of men, women and children were brought up. Some were in the extended position, some in the flexed. The bones were collected and placed in a safe mausoleum chamber provided by the Bishop Museum.

Large numbers of skeletons have been exposed by the shifting sands on all the islands. Why were the dead buried in the sand? One theory has it that the sands were once battlefields. The corpses were left where they fell and the drifting sand covered them. The only problem with that supposition is that women and children were found in the sand, and many of them had been buried in the flexed position. Besides, no weapons were ever found.

EARTH BURIALS

Some people were buried in the earth near to their homes, or even inside their homes. The graves were marked with a rectangular pavement of stones with only the borders defined. Today, Hawaiians are buried in the earth in the extended position. Royal families, however, prefer the modern mausoleum.

STONE CISTS

The stone cist was usually built near the house of the deceased. It was not a raised structure. The cist was under five inches of dirt and measured about nine feet long, two feet wide and two feet deep. The sides and ends were lined with two rows of stones, one above the other. The top was covered with four flat stones, with smaller stones to fill in the empty spaces. Six inches of dirt was used to cover the body, which was placed face up in the extended position. Since there are no special markings on these cists of stone, it is likely that there are thousands of such sites still to be discovered.

PLATFORM TOMBS

A platform tomb was found on Lanai. It was approximately two feet high, twelve feet long and fifteen feet wide. The middle was paved with small stones and coral. Underneath there were two slabs of coral stone, two by three feet in size. Below these slabs was an earth chamber three by three by four. In it was a bundle of long bones. The skulls of a man, a woman and a child were found under the bundle. With the bones was a rotted black silk handkerchief and a piece of a canoe gun-whale.

SENNIT CASKETS

This is an invention peculiar to Hawaii. Allegedly, the sennit caskets contain the bones of Liloa and Lonoikamakahiki. King Liloa was the father of the famous Hawaiian chief Umi. Lonoikamakahiki was Umi's grandson. The two caskets are similar in design, with a head, neck and a cylindrical body with no arms or legs. The neck is short and expands below into square shoulders. The body of the casket is large enough to contain the bones, trunk and limbs of the deceased. The total length of the casket is 31 inches. It is made of five-ply braid of coir fiber. Both caskets now reside in the Bishop Museum.

DEIFICATION OF A KING AFTER DEATH

The king's body was placed in the shrine part of the mua, or men's eating-house. It was wrapped in the leaves of the banana, paper mulberry and taro. It was then buried in a shallow grave about one foot below the surface. A fire was made over the full length of the grave and kept burning for ten days. Incantations were continuously recited. A Kahuna hui priest conducted the ritual. When the body was brought up, the flesh was easily removed from the bones and tossed into the sea on a kapu night. The bones were cleaned and arranged in their correct positions. Then they were bundled in tapa in the form of a human figure. The bones were placed in a sitting position. More prayers were said by the Kahuna hui and the king was transformed into a real god.

When the king died, his successor was not permitted near the area. He was in fact exiled until the ceremonies were finished. When he returned, he built a new house and a sennit casket was made for the old king's bones. This was now a shrine and the symbol of a deity. It demanded worship in the form of ritual services and offerings.

KAHILI

The Kahili was a feathered staff of state that rose nearly thirty feet. It was made of scarlet feathers and beautifully arranged on artificial branches attached to the staff. The Kahilis were made into cylinders eighteen inches in diameter and fourteen feet long. The handles were covered with tortoise shells and ivory. Said one Hawaiian: "The very grand effect of the Kahilis carried in a funeral procession will not easily be forgotten by those who have been present at such functions. The graceful forms add dignity to the stream of humanity almost as palms do to a tropical sunset. Not alone in procession—grouped about a throne or a bier they both decorate and add dignity to the place."

Timothy Green Beckley

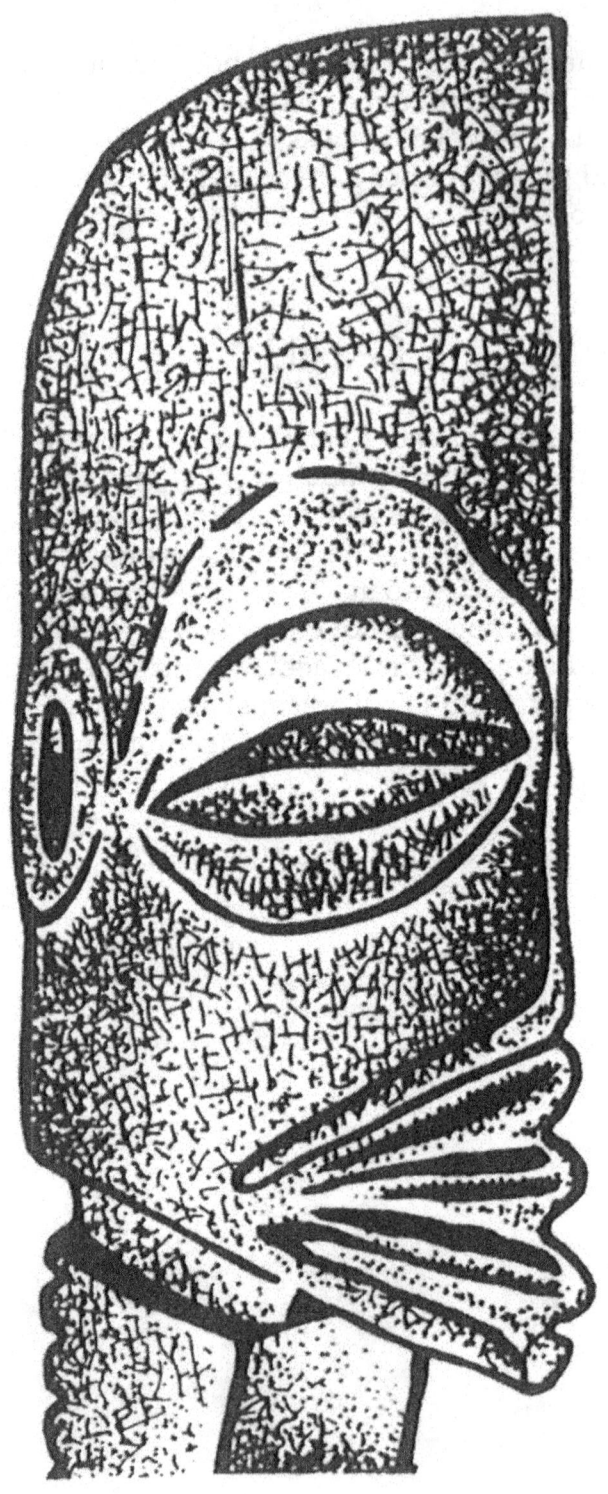

Chapter 12: The Menehune— Leprechauns of the Pacific

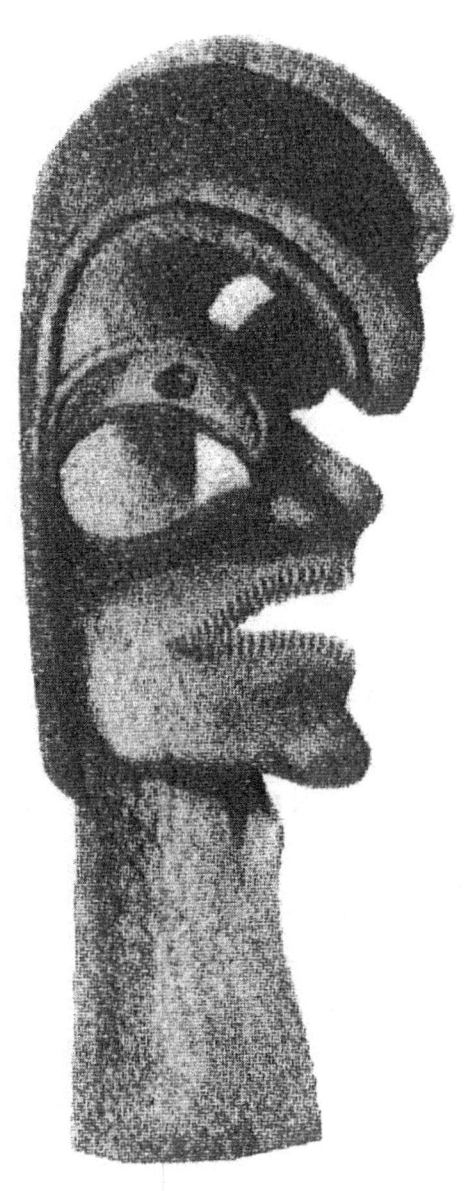

The Menehune – Leprechauns of the Pacific

Now I'm going to hit you with a blockbuster!

After hearing so much talk about the Menehune (leprechaun-like elves seen on the Islands), I am convinced that these wee people did not originate on Earth but came to our planet long ago from somewhere out in space.

Take for example the 1975 sighting of the Menehune. This episode contains the kind of details you would expect to hear from someone claiming to have encountered a being from a UFO.

When the witnesses were asked if they were telling the truth, they refused to retract any part of their story—even under promise of possible punishment from their all to skeptical parents and teachers.

There are also other similarities between the appearance of the Menehune and the sightings of spacecraft. The little people of our story show up only at night, while in the majority of cases UFOs and their alien crews also pop up under the cloak of darkness so as not to be so easily detected. The pilots of flying saucers also find it to their advantage to land in forests and other out of the way places. The Menehune, likewise, would rather keep a low profile and remain a safe distance from humans if at all possible (although they have befriended humans just as UFO crewmembers have).

This is all pretty weird stuff, but as Shakespeare once said, "There are more things in heaven and earth than are dreamt of in your philosophy." I've learned to go along with that.

--Maria H. Carta

All societies have their cultural version of the Menehune. In the Peruvian Andes, the little people are known as "Musuis," in Germany as the "Kobolds," in the Malayan mines "Chong Fus," and in England as "Tommyknockers." We here in America often refer to them as elves or fairies, and in merry ol' England, Shakespeare had his own kindred spirit identified as Puck.

Among my driving ambitions while combing the Islands for material for this book was to see a Menehune. I knew the odds were against me. For one thing, I was not a child. It would have helped me to be one. For another, I have no Hawaiian blood in me. That, too, would have helped. As things stood, my days in Hawaii ended and the little people who allegedly inhabit the forests did not show themselves to me.

I was disappointed. Some of the people I talked to insisted that the Menehune still exist and that they have been seen after dark darting about in the rich foliage. I was told that the Menehune lived in Hawaii long before the Hawaiian ancestors arrived. Their real name is *Keiki-o-ka'aina* (Children of Land). From time to time, reports of sightings are still made even today.

Walter J. Smith, owner of a tour company, says that the Wailua area is prominent in the lore of these little people. They were supposed to have lived in that area, with the Wailua Valley as their route to the sea.

The Menehune were a mysterious and industrious race of dwarf-like people perhaps two to three feet tall. They were squat and rather ugly, forever wearing dour expressions. The Menehune had many of the traits of the European elves, pixies, fairies, gnomes and trolls.

The little people were great workers, accomplishing amazing feats of energy. However, they worked only at night, and only one night on any project. Whether finished or not, the project was left forever at dawn.

The Menehune have been credited with enormous feats of engineering, including the building of the Menehune Fish Pond at Nawiliwili and the Menehune Ditch at Waimea.

It has been said that the Menehune are supernatural creatures and do not like to be seen by mortals. In spite of their dislike for humans, they do have human friends and are especially fond of children. If treated well, they will do favors for people, like building waterways, fishponds and stone temples. They are gregarious, noisy, talkative and impish. Their voices are surprisingly deep for such little fellows, but when they are all talking at once, the sound is like the low growling of dogs. They prefer to sleep all day (maybe I should have spotted them after all!). They live in lonely valleys, mountains, in caves, hollow logs and in crude huts.

According to legend, the Menehune built Poliahu Heiau, whose ruins can still be seen on Poliahu Hill. This temple, like the fishpond Menehune Ditch, had stone walls with the joints neatly fitted. All of the structures are hundreds of years old and built before it was known how to fit joints neatly together. No explanation has ever been found.

The Poliahu Heiau (temple) was built by the Menehune when the King failed to get his own people to do the job. They didn't like the strenuous labor involved. The King then made a deal with the Menehune to do the work. He promised each little one a fish. An agreement was reached.

The Menehune started their work at sunset. But during the project, one of the King's advisors thought of a bright idea. He suggested that instead of giving the little workers a big fish each, why not give them a shrimp? A shrimp is a fish, too, and there was no specification as to size. There were plenty of shrimp at Opaekaa Falls, which means Rolling Shrimp.

The King agreed. He directed his men to collect the shrimp, and at dawn he paid off the Menehune with one shrimp each. The little people were huhu (furious) but there was nothing they could do about it. They left in a huff.

The Menehune were the first people to live in Hawaii. But not long after the Polynesians arrived, they decided to leave. Most of them lived on Kaui, so they all assembled near the mouth of the river. When a floating island appeared on the horizon, they waited for it to float to shore. They leaped onto the island and floated far out to sea, over the horizon, and were never seen again.

Apparently, not all of them left. There have been sightings right there at the same river. People have seen the reddish little bodies with the hairy heads darting in and out of the underbrush.

People from all walks of life have seen the little people with the big stomachs and husky bodies. A few years ago, little four-toed footprints turned up almost everywhere. The believers in these leprechauns of the Pacific knew the little people were on the march.

The Menehune have the reputation of being serious and stern. They seem to be a scowling, fearful group. Mothers in Hawaii are likely to equate the Menehune with the bogeyman in an effort to get children to behave. But that is not fair. The Menehune are won't harm anyone if they are not molested.

In fact, their sour disposition is really the result of some bad press. In reality, they are quite playful. They enjoy pranks, love to throw stones off a cliff and then dive into the water after them. They like to spin tops, roll down hills, throw darts, box, wrestle, play tug-of-war, and glide down grassy slopes on sleds.

The Menehune are also musical. They have learned how to play mouth harps, nose flutes, and ti-leaf trumpets. And they have excellent singing voices. A woman told me, "You never see the Menehune, you hear them. They make beautiful music. But if you should see them, lie prone like the ancient Hawaiians did in the presence of their chiefs."

The woman added that if you catch a Menehune he will reveal the source of treasure. This, of course, smacks closely with the belief that the Irish leprechaun, if caught, will take you to a pot of gold.

But it is work that has made the Menehune so famous.

They have blazed forest trails, built canoes, made roads and excelled in stone masonry. Their handiwork can be found throughout the Islands. They allegedly worked in large, well-organized groups. The discipline was stern, undoubtedly because they had only one night to finish the job. It is said that they formed long lines to pass rocks from the shore, quarries or lava flows to the construction sites. They worked furiously, but if the job was not finished at sunrise, it was abandoned forever.

Little is known about their women and children, nor do we know what they wore. It's likely that they wore loincloths, tapa, or grass skirts. They like to eat yams, berries, sugarcane, squash, greens, breadfruit and poi.

They fear only two living creatures—the owl and the dog.

The population of Menehune at one time numbered over a half million on the Island of Kauai alone, and that did not include anyone under 17 years of age. Their king on one occasion forced a mass evacuation of Kauai because too many of the men were mating with Hawaiian women. It's said that only the descendants of these unions can really see the Menehune. But do they really exist? If you don't think so, consider the census of 1824, when the official responsible for taking the census noted that there were 65 Menehune living in the forest community of Laau.

Apparently, the little people are still with us. A respectable business man in Honolulu, one who is well known and held in great esteem, stated that years ago he had seen a Menehune slide down out of a tree near his home and engage him in conversation. When someone approached, the little man ran off.

If you are still skeptical, remember that many Hawaiians are still discovering fresh four-toed footprints at beaches and in pineapple fields.

Maria poses beside a plaque telling the story of the "Mo'O" said to be the guardian water spirits of the beautiful pond below. In their supernatural state, they resembled turtles or lizards, but could take on the form of beautiful young girls often seen combing their long hair. Some even believe that the Menehune assisted in the building of this pond for their fellow elemental friends (photo by Tim Beckley).

MYSTERIES OF THE MENEHUNE

One school of thought has it that the Menehune arrived at the Hawaiian Islands with the Polynesians around 750 to 1000 A.D. When the missionaries abolished the use of temples, soon after 1822, subsequent generations of Hawaiians, unaware of their origins, assumed that the Menehune built them. That may or may not be true. And the mysteries do remain. For instance, the watercourse on Kauai and the temple site on Hawaii were built of dressed, fitted stone. The usual practice had been to leave the stones in their natural shape. Did those who reached the shores of Hawaii bring stonemasons with them? Or was the sophisticated work the result of Menehune participation?

And what of the Menehune habit of completing a job overnight, or in one day? The State of Hawaii has four structures that are unfinished. I talked with a lifelong student of the Hawaiian language and it was his theory that there may have been a mistranslation of the word "day."

In ancient times, most people kept time by the lunar calendar. The "day" began at certain phases of the moon, so that a "day" could possibly last for some time. The confusion might also stem from an old Hawaiian custom that occurred when a construction project was about to begin.

Hawaiians assembled their stones, coral chunks, logs and thatching at a given site to over a period of time. When they were ready to start work, a Kahuna priest waited for the right moment when the phase of the moon signaled a new "day." Then he would give his permission to start building. If the structure was not finished by the time the moon entered an unfavorable phase, work was stopped and the building was left unfinished forever.

MENEHUNE LEGENDS

The prodigious workers known as Menehune once took a spring from its rocky bed, wrapped it in ti-leaves and carried it to the lowlands so that the villagers would have water for their taro patches.

The Menehune only ate the whole of any food so that no part would be left, as there would be if they feasted on pork or a large fish. So they ate bananas, poi, small fish and shrimp. They planted their bananas, taro and sweet potatoes in small hollow places on cliffs. You can still see the trails they made on the cliffs of Kauai. Hawaiian men will tell you that when they spend the night in the uplands, they roast bananas in hot coals. They don't really need to eat the bananas, but they know how much the Menehune like them. The Hawaiians sit very still in the dark, and pretty soon they see long pointed poles reach out from the blackness and spear the bananas.

There are many stones in Hawaii that look suspiciously like people. This is why: Once there was a boastful Menehune who bragged that he could catch the moon. His Menehune friends laughed at him when he climbed a hill to accomplish his impossible task. The moon was high in the heavens when he came down empty-handed. For his boastfulness, he was turned into a stone as punishment.

Before dawn, the group of Menehune stood near their great fish catch. They had been at it all night, hauling in fish after fish. They were little fish, the kind they could eat and not leave anything behind. They planned to salt some of them so that they would have food for many nights.

The sun came up. The group slept, but left guards to watch their fish. All through the day the guards were nervous. They heard strange sounds. There were whisperings and every once in a while they heard stone sliding. These sounds did not come from the beach, or from the mountain slope. Then one guard said that there was a narrow tunnel through the mountain and that someone was coming through it.

All the guards listened. They determined that many were coming and that they were evil spirits who wanted to steal the fish. All of the Menehune were awakened and they had a meeting. The chief said he had a plan. "Let us tunnel into the mountain and take those spirits by surprise."

There were so many Menehune and they worked so diligently that they tunneled deep into the mountain in no time at all. They reached the narrow passage where the evil spirits were, and as each spirit passed through the gap, he was set upon by a Menehune warrior and slain. The fish were saved and the little people had food for many nights.

True story? Who knows? But one thing is certain: You can go to Ha'ena, to that same mountain, and see the dry cave that reaches deep inside.

RECENT SIGHTING

The Menehune have been seen elsewhere in the South Pacific. This report was printed in the *Fiji Times* on July 19, 1975:

Students at the Lautoka Methodic Mission School reported seeing about eight mysterious little creatures in reeds near the school. The human figures were about two feet tall and were covered with black hair. When the children approached them, they fled into a bush.

The excitement brought more students and teachers into the area. People hurried over from nearby Lautoka Fijian School. Scores of neighbors rushed to the scene. It was theorized that the little people had jumped into a pit near the bush, but the head teacher, Sadamand Narayan, said that they couldn't be found in there.

For days afterward, dozens of people gathered at the pit in the hope of seeing the little men. They sat there for hours holding sticks and torches in case they were attacked.

Head teacher Narayan told a team of reporters from the *Fiji Times* that he had threatened the students with punishment if he found out they were lying. "But they remained firm in whatever they said about the mysterious figures," he said.

The students who actually saw the figures were Paras Ram, 14, David Keshwan, 14, Jonathan Surendra, 13, Viliane Kuglamu, 10, Ruci Muricuba, 11, and Naumi Tuyakaya, 10. They were on their way home after school. Ruci said, "I saw his white gleaming eyes and black hair. I was frightened."

Naumi said, "One showed me his teeth and then ran away."

David said that he made an effort to speak to them, but they ran away.

A villager named Peniasi Tora stated that his forefathers had often talked about coming to Fiji and finding little people already living there.

Do the Menehune of Hawaii really exist? I can't answer that question, but when I talked to Hawaiians about them, I was struck by their sincerity in believing that they do live off the beaten path. My informants were educated, sophisticated and held responsible positions on the Islands. They were rational. They told me that the Menehune were there to serve Hawaiians. They said that there are many cases on record in which a Menehune or two finished a job during the night that someone had left undone during the day. Shrimp and bananas and other tasty morsels were left for the little workers and the food was always gone the next day.

These people I spoke with looked me straight in the eye. They weren't lying.

How can I doubt them?

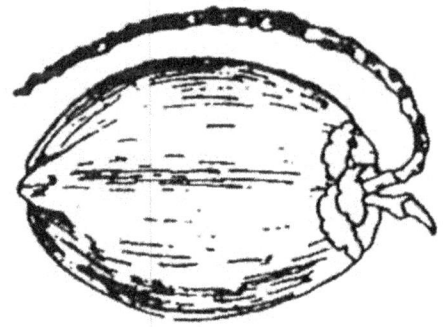

The hula dance is an unspoken form of communication between Islanders often associated with love (photo by Tim Beckley).

Chapter 13:
Hawaii's Mysterious Madame Pele— Fire Goddess and Phantom Hitchhiker

Hawaii's Mysterious Madame Pele – Fire Goddess and Phantom Hitchhiker

During our quest, we met several very "special" people who came to us to share their love of Hawaii. These individuals realize that the Islands have a unique spirituality about them. One of our new friends is a delightful young lady name Aja Millage, who discussed her belief in the powers of the God Neptune and in the existence of Madame Pele. Many feel the Goddess Pele still watches over Hawaii, sort of like a guardian angel appearing in human form to warn her loved ones when danger is about to strike.

Aja is the personification of the New Age mentality that is sweeping the country, showing her concern and love for all living things and holding a belief that everything in the universe exists for a definite purpose and is interconnected.

Aja has had numerous UFO sightings, including the observation of a huge cigar-shaped mothership that appeared in the sky shortly before our arrival. She matter-of-factly accepts that otherworldly craft are visiting Earth and are piloted by beings much like us, whom she calls our "Space Brothers and Sisters." Aja believes that these space people are here to offer guidance and support, and are related to the spirits that have long made Hawaii their home.

Pat McKinley is also fascinated by the appearance of strange shapes and forms in the heavens. She sees UFOs as being symbolic of a gradual change that is taking place in our world, including a blending of the "old" and the "new" traditions and resulting in a more holistic society. To Pat and Aja, the "ways of the Kahuna" are still very important. They are not meant to be lost or destroyed by those with "closed minds." Both sense there is a " higher purpose" in UFOs, and that these craft will lead us to more spiritual ways in the years just ahead.

Kalani Hanohano knows all about the "flying gods," going so far, in years past, as to publish an excellent newsletter.

FULL MOON: A REPORT FROM THE ISLANDS was unsurpassed in its excellent references to the unexplainable phenomena of Hawaii, historically as well as in recent times. Since he is a seasoned journalist, a qualified researcher, and foremost a pure Hawaiian, Kalani, better than anyone else, is able to piece together folklore with valid scientific evidence for the existence of that which others "not so aware" might tend to scoff at.

Mentioned previously, Joseph Iida is convinced the Gods are still very much with us. As evidence, he claims to have encountered Madame Pele in human form on two occasions. Both times, she appeared as the harbinger of disaster. All those we encountered wished us to express, on their behalf, the true universal meaning of love, which they feel is still very evident in Hawaii, a land they insist will help usher in a New Age of enlightenment and magic on this planet not witnessed since the days of Atlantis and the masterful wisdom of the Kahuna.

After our journey was over, we could not help but feel sad. Our plans call for us to return to this paradise of beauty and enchantment that has given Hawaii the well-deserved reputation of being our most mystical state. We hope you can travel there yourself and feel the unique energy that abounds throughout the Islands.

--Maria H. Carta

Devotees of Madame Pele occasionally call for her to return to the volcano for a visit. This is the prayer they repeat at such times. It is a prayer you can say anytime for protection and to ward off evil.

O pele la ko'u akua
Pele is my deity

Miha ka lani, miha ka honua
Silent is the heaven, silent is the earth

E kapu, I kapu kai ka 'awa
Make tabu the 'awa with a ceremonial sea bath

Ka 'awa, ka 'awa o ola
The 'awa, the 'awa of life

E loa ka wai apu
Make long the water in the coconut shell cup

E Pele-honua-mea, E la!
Pele-honua-mea, arise!

Eia ka palala, he pule
Here is the gift, a prayer

O ka wahine I Kilauea
O woman of Kilauea

Wahine o ka lani
Woman of heaven

Wahine lole kohi ahi
Woman in fiery apparel

Eia mai ka 'awa
Here is the 'awa

Eia mai ka moha pua'a
Here is the sacrificial pig.

MADAME PELE'S POWERS

Madame Pele is the Polynesian goddess of fire. Many Hawaiians consider her to be very real. Many more who pride themselves on being "civilized and sophisticated" would nevertheless think twice about doing anything to offend her. When she first came to Hawaii, legend has it Madame Pele took up residence in the crater on Diamond Head, which is the famous landmark at the end of Waikiki Beach. When the Islands had their first leader, Kamehameha, she moved to Kilauea. She favored the great leader and took his side during his early conquests, causing the volcano to erupt at the right moment to cut off enemy troops with her lava.

Madame Pele is actually said to live in the pit crater of Halemaumau, which is in the center of Kilauea's caldera (cauldron). She is both loved and feared. You do not offend Pele. Chances are that nothing will happen to you, but then . . . who knows? Something just may happen.

For instance, Hawaiians tell the tourists again and again that it is bad to take chunks of lava or rocks from Kilauea. But they do anyway. They take Pele's property to use as a paperweight or decoration. Then they learn their mistake.

The superintendents of Hawaii Volcanoes National Park and Haleakala National Park, or the mayor, receive dozens of packages every year. Inside are chunks of lava or rocks, and the letter with them usually reads something like this: "I've been plagued by bad luck ever since I brought these home. Please return them to Madame Pele at the volcano."

Regardless of the form she materializes with, many Hawaiians still believe in the powers of Madame Pele who appears as a beautiful woman with flowing red hair, (see insert) or an aged crone, just before disaster strikes. (photo by Tim Beckley)

MADAME PELE'S WARNINGS

The old Hawaiian legend has it that shortly before an eruption, Madame Pele makes an appearance in human form. This is her way of warning the people to beware. On May 14, 1924, at Waiohinu in the southernmost province of Ka'u on the Big Island, the *Honolulu Advertiser* reported that a resident had seen a tall, strange but beautiful woman dressed in white and with flowing red hair.

At the time, there was very little tourism in Hawaii, and natives tended to know each other. The individual was a stranger. Several other people reported seeing the same unusual woman walking along a country lane. She spoke to no one and was not seen again.

Four days later, on May 18, Kilauea, which had been rumbling for nearly a month, exploded. Huge, towering clouds of dust rose more than 20,000 feet above the crater. An eight-ton boulder was lifted into the air and deposited a quarter of a mile away.

Madame Pele had given her warning.

MADAME PELE'S VARIOUS FORMS

When Pele makes her appearance it is always as a female. Sometimes she looks like a beautiful young maiden; at other times, like an old crone. People who encounter an old woman on the road are always careful to treat her with great respect. Pele has also appeared as a woman covered with flames, or flames in the shape of a woman.

THE GODDESS APPEARS... AND DISAPPEARS

Mary Kawena Pukui has been studying Hawaiian legends for these many years and recounts an experience she had when she was a child. The anthropologist says that she saw a fireball moving slowing from the Kilauea Crater and rising up the side of giant Mauna Loa. Her older sister and other relatives also saw the strange object. Attempts have been made to explain it as ball lightning, or perhaps a UFO. Hawaiians saw it as just another manifestation of Madame Pele.

Honolulu papers in another case told of a couple on vacation on the Big Island. While driving from Kona through Ka'u and on to Kilauea, they picked up a woman on a barren stretch of highway above South Point. She sat in the backseat and said nothing. After several miles of driving, the husband turned around to offer her a cigarette. The woman was not there. They had not made any stops since picking her up, but she had vanished.

A few days later, Kilauea Iki erupted. It was one of the most spectacular eruptions in history.

THE PHANTOM HITCHIKER

From time to time witnesses come forth with strange stories of meeting Madame Pele on the roads near the volcano. The most disturbing part about these witnesses is that they are all quite normal in every respect and not given to flights of fancy. They are usually quite shaken up by their experiences.

Recently a man was traveling from Kamuela to Hilo. It was about eight o'clock at night and he was on a lonely stretch of Saddle Road. He suddenly saw a woman standing beside the road. He pulled over. He asked her where she was going and she said, "To Hilo." He gave her a lift. She sat in the backseat. She was quiet. A few miles later he turned to say something to her, but she was gone. Frightened, he floored the gas pedal and sped into Hilo to tell someone that he had had Madame Pele in his car.

In my travels through Hawaii, I have spoken to residents who have told me that it is not at all unusual for motorists driving around the volcano to see an old woman or a beautiful, younger woman in the area. When she is picked up, she always insists on riding in the backseat. She tells the driver where she wants to go, then falls asleep. When the driver reaches the destination, he turns to arouse the woman, but she is gone.

I spoke to a bus driver who had a frightening experience. He told me that late one night he was driving his bus on the volcano road when he spotted an elderly woman waiting at the bus stop. He picked her up. She was the only passenger on the bus and she told him where she would like to get off. When he reached the spot, he stopped the bus and opened the door. He waited for the woman to get off, but she didn't. He turned to see where she was. She was gone. The experience scared him so much that he quit his job.

Our friend, Joseph Iida, has seen Pele twice and says he can tell from the way she is dressed that what kind of disaster is likely to transpire.

"Dressed as a *white ghost,* it means that there will soon be volcanic eruption," he contends.

"If she appears in a *long cape* similar to the one worn by the late Hawaiian kings, you can rest assured that there will be a tidal wave or hurricane."

On the other hand, if Pele is *dressed in black*, Joseph feels that "sudden death" or a "great tragedy" is not likely to be more than 24 hours away.

Joseph Iida feels somehow that the ability to see Madame Pele is inherited. "This type of thing usually runs in the family. My grandfather was stopped on the road by her and told he shouldn't pass. Later, he found there was some sort of disaster just up ahead. Another time, the spirits spoke to him and told him where some old Hawaiian silver pieces were buried. He found them exactly as he was directed.

Not too long ago, Joseph was driving with three young men when he saw Pele at the side of the road. She was dressed in a long cloak and was soaking wet. "We went on our way fishing and I said we should turn around. I told them that there was going to be trouble in three days. I was so certain about this that I tried to contact my wife, who had gone away fishing on the other side of the island. When I couldn't reach her myself, I had the police get in touch with her to tell her to return home before the rains and wind hit. Luckily, she got back before the road washed out.

"Funny thing is, there was considerable damage all around our house. The roof of the two homes on either side of us were blown right off and one of them even damaged our back fence, but our house wasn't touched at all." Proof once again that Madame Pele never harms those who believe in her!

WHO IS MADAME PELE?

She is a goddess who legend has it came from Tahiti to live in Hawaii with her seven brothers and six sisters. All of the children were experts in some form of sorcery and in the hula. Pele can assume many body and object forms. She can change herself into a blazing flame, a beautiful young girl or an old hag.

When Madame Pele is a beautiful woman, she is given to ferocious tantrums of rage and jealousy. In a snit, she can stamp her foot on the ground and cause it to tremble with earthquakes. Cracks will suddenly appear in the soil and there will be huge torrents of molten lava that will chase those who have angered her. Sometimes the fire goddess will ride the first wave of liquid rock, screaming oaths and throwing flaming boulders at her enemies. This is the side of Madame Pele that is seen most often. Her most prominent emotions are all negative—anger, jealousy, bad temper and sulkiness.

PELE'S VENGEANCE AGAINST A TV SHOW

In 1974, "Hawaii Five-O" was a popular television series. A segment was being filmed on the Big Island. Production, however, was delayed by heavy rains. The TV crew went to Waimea, where there had been a drought for three weeks. But as soon as the crew arrived, rain came down in torrents. The film crew then hurried to Hilo, where it was sunny. But change came swiftly, and it rained hard. The filming was delayed for weeks.

What happened? The Honolulu newspapers had the answer. They reported that the film crew had eaten some ohelo berries without first getting Pele's permission and without offering some of the berries to her. The men had also taken some rocks and lava as souvenirs. These actions had angered the fire goddess. You might think it was coincidence, but many of the Hawaiians I spoke to about the incident are convinced that Madame Pele exacted her vengeance against the film crew by making it rain wherever they went.

THE FIREBALLS OF HAWAII

The longest running east rift event (eruption) in Kilauea's recorded history began on January 3, 1983. There were about 26 major events and a number of lesser ones. At that time, both Kilauea and Mauna Loa erupted. It was during this time that National Park Ranger Kepa Maly witnessed at midnight a fireball traveling from Kilauea to Mauna Loa. Kepa Maly is a cultural expert who was raised by a pure Hawaiian family on Lanai.

Maly said that traditional lore holds that Madame Pele at times travels in her popoahi or fireball when she wants to assert her domain. He said that a week earlier there was a snowfall on Mauna Loa. Some experts interpreted that as snow deities trying to push Pele from the volcano.

Maly said that Madame Pele persevered. She traveled to Kilauea to reassert her power, then returned to Mauna Loa. "It was a legend in life rather than just another scientific story. Our own Park Service people actually saw this flash either leave Kilauea or pass by Mauna Loa."

Robert Decker, chief scientist at the U.S. Geological Survey's Hawaiian Volcano Observatory, thought the flash was unrelated to volcano activity. He said the fountaining of lava stopped a few hours after the fireball crossed the night sky.

Timothy Green Beckley

Many native Hawaiians believe strongly that guardian spirits protect them, their loved ones, as well as their homes from negativity, and can bring them good luck. Such a spirit is seen here with arms raised to the heavens in front of a hut by one of the original Kahuna High Priests to perform a sacred ritual. (photo by Tim Beckley)

PELE'S FIREBALL DISGUISE

The sport of chiefs at one time was sledding. Madame Pele took the form of an old woman and challenged the young chief Kahawali to a contest. He refused. She immediately took the form of a fireball and chased him down the hill. Somehow, he managed to escape to another island. Another chief, racing along with the fireball, made the mistake of getting caught ahead of it. When he looked back, Pele in her fire-form caught up and overwhelmed him with lava. This was the fate of many others who failed to recognize Pele in whatever disguise she used. It also happened to those who violated her taboos or did something else to make her angry.

In many cases Pele would appear at someone's door as a very old and crippled woman. The residents would take her to a hospital for treatment. Then later she would vanish in a burst of flame, doing nothing to her benefactors because they tried to help her.

The spun volcanic glass that drifts with the trade winds is referred to as "Pele's hair." Her tears are drops of burning lava that fall after fountaining.

In modern stories about Madame Pele she is most often seen in red. Here dresses are red. Her skin is fiery and glowing. Her hair is red. Only once was she seen in black. On one occasion, she was picked up in a car as an old woman, then transformed herself into a beautiful girl before vanishing. At another time, someone touched her and reported later that her skin was hot.

Among her many forms is that of a ball of fire that is smaller than the moon. When the ball is seen in the night sky, people are likely to say, "The old woman of the Pit is going to her other home."

MYSTERY OF THE AKUALELE

In my travels through the Big Island and other Hawaiian areas, I was struck by the number of witnesses who have seen the akualele, or "flying ghosts." Most of the people I questioned said that they had seen these apparitions at least once, that often these akualele appear as a huge red-eyed ghost dog. The flying ghosts appear as fire. Many Hawaiians carefully avoid going into areas where the ghosts have been seen. One writer by the name of J.K. Mokumai reported on a strange fireball sighting occurring in the Mauna Loa area on the Island of Oahu. He stated:

"It was customary that when a company of people passed time away on the Ewa side of Mauna Loa, facing the edge of that hill, at eventide, a fire would be seen crawling on the edge of the cliff and drop down on that hill. It was a rocket. Your writer had seen it himself, and being too young to know better, we children shouted aloud, 'Oh, see the fire with a head in front of it and a long tail!' We children liked it, we older ones, and we were always eager to see this flying object. We questioned each other about this flying fire. We used to form a group to watch it. For two or three nights there was no sign of it, and on the fifth night every one of the boys that came, including the writer, saw its head and eyes. It was as red as fire and frightful. We screamed aloud in fear and later learned the truth. It was fed and was tame. It took the form of a man and went up there to look for food."

A caretaker at one of the active volcanoes states that in one of the caves along the cliffs lives an akualele and that every so often it comes out and flies about. On one occasion a young girl with a group of people in a car was asked to chant in the area. She did so, and while she was chanting a bright ball of fire appeared and approached the car. The occupants were so frightened that they sped away—with the ball of fire flying next to them. Eventually it veered off and returned to the cave.

FIREBALLS REPRESENT DISHARMONY

Fireballs nearly always are seen at night, and when one is seen outside a home, it usually means that inside there may be disharmony, jealousy and hatred. According to the people I spoke with, the akualele can be stopped and destroyed by swearing at it. They explode at such times, but don't harm anyone. Instead, they break up into small flames, each moving and writhing on its own, indicating that these puffs of light are animate objects.

In a recent case, which was told to me by an elderly resident, a marriage had taken place that was not acceptable to one side of the family. There were racial and religious differences. One of the husband's cousins brought in a kahuna-pule-'umi, who recited a prayer, the result of which brought a fireball to the bride and groom's house. Neighbors saw the bright object fall on the house. The old Kahuna priest, however, could not properly execute the prayer because it required long breath control. He collapsed and was rushed to a hospital, where he lay dying.

The fireball had no real effect on the house. The elderly man told me that it was not because the Kahuna failed in his prayer but because the young groom was the descendant of the Ma'iola god and had not needed to swear to render the fireball impotent.

In another case told to me there was an 88-year-old woman living at Maunalani Heights on Oahu who said that in the 1940s she was startled by a bright light at her front door. It was a fireball. She said that someone in her family was against her. She prayed for divine guidance, and in a dream that night she learned that one family member was jealous of her.

I also learned that a male Hawaiian living in the Kailua are on the Kona Coast of Hawaii said that when he was a young man, a fireball of bright yellow light crashed through the air and flew over and under some trees. He was just about to swear at it when the akualele smashed into a tree and exploded into lots of small flames.

Some Hawaiians feel that the sight of a fireball is a bad omen and that one should turn back from wherever one is going, or should stop whatever one is doing.

Fireball witnesses are apparently plentiful. I had no trouble finding people who had seen them. One young man told me that while he was driving down Old Pali Road on Oahu a fireball passed slowly in front of his car. The engine died. But as soon as the fireball left, the engine kicked into life again.

In another case two men were driving along the same Old Pali Road when a fireball appeared. The driver stopped the car, got out and started to swear. The fireball broke up into small balls. The driver told me that those flaming fragments became little mythical men called e'epa.

A 17-year-old female told me that she once saw a fireball hovering above her head at about fifty feet. It spun in flight and then crashed to the ground. A man and his wife spotted a huge luminous blue fireball that fell almost at her their feet. When the wife tried to touch it, it rose up and flew away.

To sum up what I learned about these strange fiery objects: they can be sent by someone human, they can be stopped by swearing, they leave sparks behind while flying, and vary in color from red to orange and white to blue and orange to white. And they are omens.

To learn still more about fireballs as related to Kahuna beliefs, I consulted a Kahuna friend who apparently knew everything about Hawaii and its mythology.

He told me that, "The akualele were once *kino lau* (multiple bodies) of gods and demigods. Their mission was mostly to punish the people who broke the laws of the land. Later, these akualele became captured spirits who were of less importance than gods and demigods and were used mainly by men against men. The power shifted from the domain of gods to he control of men."

In any case, it's my guess that Madame Pele approves no matter who controls the fireballs. Furthermore, many residents feel she will continue to be seen, and are fearful that there will be a disastrous eruption in the not too distant future.

Hopefully, her appearance in human form may, once again, save many lives!

Its a huff and a puff, but author Tim Beckley manages to scale the sides of Haleakala crater in an attempt to knock on the door of the volcano Goddess Pele...unfortunately, she did not anwser! (Photo by Penny Melis)

Chapter 14: Captain Nancy and the Mystical Powers of Dolphins

Captain Nancy and the Mystical Powers of Dolphins

The boat pitched back and forth as we climbed aboard. There was a bit of a breeze out on the ocean, and it took us a few minutes to get our water legs.

Psychic Penny Melis and her daughter Mayven had joined me on my return trip to the Islands. Being a sensitive whose roots lay with the shamanic community, Penny wanted to experience for herself the mysticism of the Hawaiian culture, and in particular undergo her own close encounter with the friendly aquatic creatures that populate the waters of the Pacific.

Mayven had seen dolphins on television and in the movies, and even though she was not an experienced swimmer—hell, she was only four at the time of our expedition—she genuinely pushed her mother to take her on the adventure of a lifetime, one that would certainly grow with her as she matured. To say that Mayven took to water is hardly the way to explain her ability to adapt to an unknown venue. She was bobbing and weaving in the clear blue ocean, safely secured in a life jacket and held in the experienced hands of a seasoned swimmer. The captain of our sea-faring vessel later commented on how she felt almost certain more dolphins followed our boat than was usual, picking up the friendly vibes of the child as well as the even temperament of those who had come onboard to make friendly contact with another species.

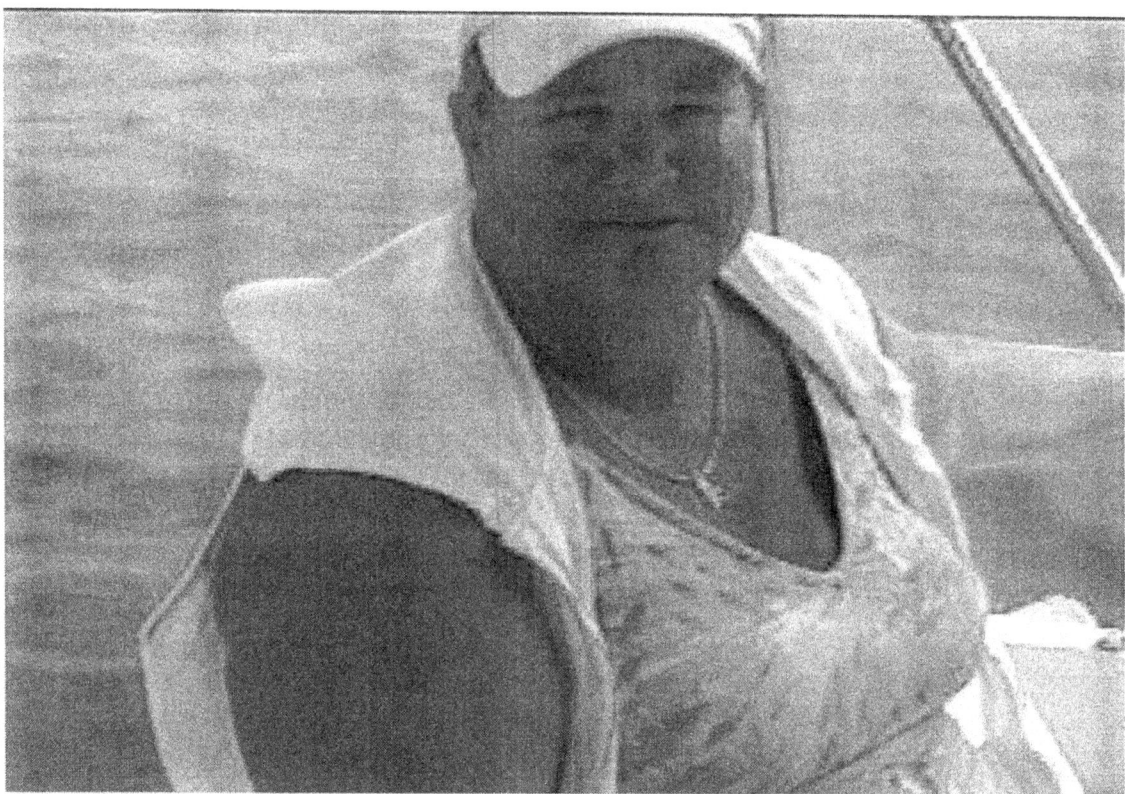

Accustomed to being on the open seas, Captain Nancy of Dolphin Journey seems to have a sixth sense for determining when these beloved creatures are nearby and anxious to swim along side their newly found human friends. With a degree in Oceanography, Captain Nancy is also a master of relating the metaphysical experiences of those who have entered the aquatic realm of the dolphins if only for a brief while (Photo by Tim Beckley).

Captain Nancy, as she prefers to be called, has degrees in both geology and oceanography and a solid academic background that serves her well in her current profession as a seafaring tour guide in Hawaii. But her real expertise involves the kinds of things they don't teach you in any college or university. Captain Nancy is, as you will see in the following chapter, one who not only swims with the dolphins but also speaks their language.

The story begins sort of tragically. It was 1994, and Captain Nancy had suffered injuries from four separate car accidents and was not fully recovered.

"I wasn't doing very well physically," she said. "I was feeling a lot of neurological challenges."

After attending a seminar on the local dolphins in Kona, Hawaii, she experimented with swimming with the creatures.

"I just felt tremendously better," Captain Nancy said, "after one week of swimming with the dolphins. I stayed for another two and a half months and then never went home."

CONVERSING IN THE WORLD OF VIBRATIONS

In the ensuing years, she learned that the dolphins do indeed have their methods for communicating with human beings.

"All you have to do is think a thought," Captain Nancy explained, "and your thoughts carry a vibration. The dolphins are very sensitive to vibrations, and they will pick up whatever vibratory energy you're putting out. Then they will send you a vibration back. It's as simple as any other vibrations we're picking up from humans or other animals. In my case, I just sort of know. I just get an answer when I've asked a question. The thought process comes back very clearly, very distinctly, of 'This is your answer.'

"It's changed my life completely," she added. "I'm a very different person than I was before I swam with the dolphins. It really opens your heart."

A TRANSFORMATION OF THE SOUL

The changes made by the dolphin experience may even penetrate to the cellular level, according to Captain Nancy.

"My belief is that even my DNA has changed tremendously," she said. "I've softened greatly. I'm much more compassionate and understanding of people than I was before I came out here and worked with the dolphins. I have information that gets 'downloaded,' the best way that I can explain it, that I don't know where I ever learned it. It just shows up in my mind."

When Captain Nancy does her briefing of her passengers each morning before her tour sets out, she characterizes what she typically says as "dolphin channeling."

"Every time I do a briefing on my boat," she said, "it's a different set of information. And I know that that's information that the dolphins want any particular group to hear."

Captain Nancy said her dog Pluto also communicates with the dolphins by imitating the noises they make.

"He can hear their vibrations and their sounds," she said, "that we can't hear. So he's learned to mimic their noise."

PRECOGNITIVE CREATURES OF THE SEA

The dolphins also seem to be aware of future events.

"The days when the tsunami was coming," Captain Nancy said, "two Christmases before, we had very strange days out here. Everybody was back at the harbor saying, 'Gosh, the dolphins are acting peculiarly.' We didn't know what was happening. We just knew that *something* was happening. The same thing happened when the Iraq war broke out, a similar kind of strange behavior. I don't always necessarily know what that behavior is going to translate into. In my case, it's more like I just know something's wrong."

At the time the interview was conducted, in the spring of 2006, the dolphins were pretty much in a state of gentle contentment.

"We haven't seen any unusual behaviors," Captain Nancy said, "in the last few weeks that I would say was pertaining to something special. What we mostly find, and what's very interesting, is how they change from person to person. Sometimes they'll start to get very close, what we call 'kissing distance.' And there are other days when we have a harder time finding the dolphins, and when we do, they don't want to interact with these people. It's always curious to me."

DOLPHINS AS MATCHMAKERS

The dolphins often react with Captain Nancy's passengers in a way that seems perfectly suited to the passengers' specific needs.

"We had a wonderful lady who was having some relationship challenges," Captain Nancy said. "She had her own set ideas. She really wasn't certain about this idea of communicating with dolphins, but she would try it. Basically, she went out with the dolphins and finished the swim just buzzing. She could feel her whole body vibrating. The end of the story was that she ended up meeting the man of her dreams that night and falling in love and soon after got married and had a child. She had been just about to marry somebody else and was sort of 'close-minded,' but she came out here and thought, 'Gosh, I wonder what the dolphins have to say?' She was headed left and she suddenly turned right. We hear stories like that from people all the time."

Captain Nancy explained further about what she felt had happened to the woman.

"She went back to the mainland," Captain Nancy said, "and just absolutely fell in love with this man and said that it was all so clear when she was with the dolphins, that this was generated by the shift that she needed to make within herself, to be ready for this more perfect man for her. It was an internal shift that happened within her that prepared her to be with somebody who was more appropriate to her new energy field that went with the dolphin experience."

A GENTLE NUDGE TO LOOK BACK

In addition to their matchmaking skills, the dolphins are playful and seem to enjoy a good joke now and then. They can also perhaps impart a valuable lesson at the same time. Captain Nancy told the story of a family she took out on her boat one day.

"The mother and the children were having this amazing dolphin experience," Captain Nancy recalled. "But the father kept coming back to the boat and saying, 'Nancy, I haven't seen the dolphins.' I'd watched this dolphin following him all day long, right behind his hip. I said, 'The dolphins are right behind you. Just look behind you.'

"He went off and swam again and here's this dolphin right behind him. And he still came back to the boat and said, 'I haven't seen a single dolphin. My family's having this amazing experience, with the dolphins so close, but they're not coming to me.' So finally he gave up. I just couldn't help but ask him, 'What is there in your life that's behind you that you don't want to look at?' Because he wouldn't look behind him to see the dolphins. Sometimes they're little tricksters and they play games with people like that."

THE JOURNEY TO THE LIGHT

Along with the humor, however, there are also tears.

"One of my saddest stories," Captain Nancy said, "is about a little boy named Eli. He was very sick with cancer. He was about six years old, and he and his mother and I were out swimming with the dolphins. When you're swimming with the dolphins, when the sun is shining, you see this gorgeous light that looks like this vortex. And I kept getting it in my head, 'Tell this lady that when Eli dies, he's going into this light.' I kept thinking, 'I can't tell this woman her child is going to die. She's brought him here to be healed with the dolphins.'"

The message to Captain Nancy's head persisted, growing louder and louder.

"Finally, I tried very tactfully," she said, "to say to her, 'You see this light? This is what Eli is going to go to when he passes on and makes his transition.' So about six months after they were here, I started to get emails from them saying Eli isn't doing very well, but he wakes up every morning from a dream, saying 'Mommy, Mommy, don't wake me up. I want to stay with the dolphins. I keep dying, but the dolphins keep saving me.'

"About a month after that," Captain Nancy continued, "Eli did make his transition. His mother said that up to the moment that he was passing on, he kept saying, 'Mommy, it's okay. I'm going to go into the light with the dolphins.' They made a stained glass window in honor of Eli with the dolphins swimming up into the light. His family was very touched. His mother said the most calming thing she remembered was swimming with me and the dolphins and me showing her the light and reminding her that Eli is just going to the light. I think, had I never said that to her, and if I hadn't gotten that message in my head—it would never occur to me to tell a mother, 'Your child is going to die and go into the light.' But that's some of the communications that the dolphins give."

THE DOLPHINS HAVE A MISSION

The dolphins have come to Earth as messengers, Captain Nancy believes.

"They really are our brothers and sisters of the sea," she said. "They're more intelligent than we are. They truly come as messengers. Some people call them 'the angels of the sea.' Why? You'd have to ask the dolphins.

"We get people that want so badly to connect with them," she went on. "I think that is the dolphins 'calling' people. It's the dolphins' mission, and it's why they're here on the planet. When they get a significant number of people that have been touched with this energy that they are evoking through their sonar, then indeed I think we're going to see that New World Order that we've been talking about. It's beginning to happen. It's beginning to form.

"The dolphins and the whales are both a very critical piece, connected in with the ETs, and it's all a divine triangle of helping mankind to evolve into our next level of evolution. That's the energy that the dolphins are trying to give us, by connecting with us, 'sonar-ing' us, implanting information for people to live a life in more harmony. A world of peace, everything that we all dream to be—that's what the dolphins say you can have every day."

To contact Captain Nancy Sweatt and make reservations for a dolphin swim of your own, call 808-329-3030 or 808-384-1218. Or email her at: info@dolphinjourneys.com

Timothy Green Beckley

Hawaiian tike images or idols are known worldwide. The artists who make them are remarkable craftsmen who spend days working the wooden images that often represent good and bad luck as well as self told tales. Here we see such an artist working on a tike that now belongs to the author and sits on the tike bar in his office. Often such figures are placed in front of a home to ward off negativity and to attract positive energies.
(photo by Tim Beckley)

Chapter 15:
The Spiritual and Psychic Quest of Penny Melis

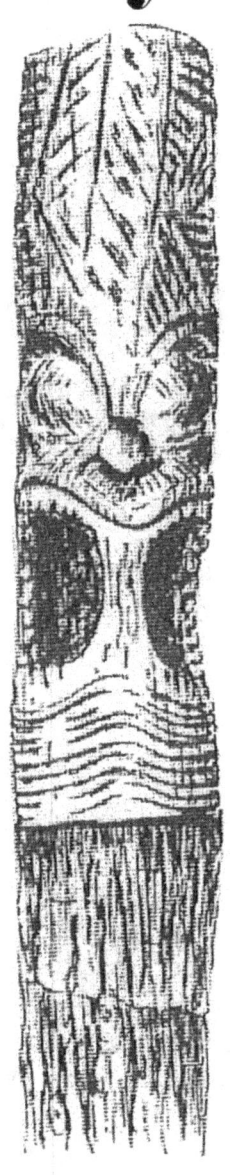

The Spiritual and Psychic Quest of Penny Melis

When Tim Beckley asked me to contribute my impressions of our trip—his second journey to the Islands, my first—I had an overwhelming desire to do the best job possible in getting across the mental as well as spiritual images of what I absorbed so that those joining this literary sojourn could understand why I felt it would be advantageous for me to go along with my daughter on this rather lengthy trip from the East Coast of the United States to the far reaches of the Pacific.

For you see, basically, the supernatural comes easy to me. After being exiled from the Carolinas, my great, great grandmother—being the product of a Native American raid—settled in Salem, Massachusetts. Unfortunately, the move was during a shameful and horrifying chapter in American history. My ancestors suffered many trials during the hysteria and three were hanged for witchcraft. However, there was a survivor who married and secretly moved to central Pennsylvania. Soon the town of Penn Woods became a haven for the weary and persecuted.

A GIFTED LINEAGE

My grandmother was the product of a mixed breed and a blueblood from Scotland-Ireland who utilized the natural ways of the land, no doubt inbred into her subconscious by those ancestors who had also been so motivated by that which existed above and on the land. My grandmother was born with a cowl over her face. In a time when medicine was young, she was able to survive the odds of death and prove the old wives tale true.

Today, I celebrate my proud lineage and use elements of both Wiccan and Native American practices in my daily life and spiritual beliefs. I found that this mixture creates harmony with nature and the environment. Additional insights have come from my father's Greek ancestry. In the July 2006 issue of **FATE Magazine**, Tim Beckley described our psychic perceptions of our trip to pick up on the historical vibrations of the famed Oracle at Delphi.

I should also explain that my grandmother on my father's side was a visionary and was said to have the gift of second sight. Many years ago, when she was young, gypsies had come to her town. In order to get rid of them, she showed them that she was not fearful and that she was indeed a force in the village. The gypsies gave grandmother the sight because they felt she was truly strong enough to handle the power and maybe they felt it was a curse. My grandmother eventually foretold her own death.

Having this affinity with "another world," invisible to most, I felt traveling to Hawaii with Tim would further heighten my connections with other dimensions and realms. The awareness of the Hawaiian shamanic culture did much to expand my perceptions, and my communications with dolphins proved that we are not the only intelligent species to inhabit this planet. More about the dolphins later.

THE GODDESS PELE

Pele is a red-haired woman who might appear on the side of the road as you approach the volcanoes. She usually accepts rides from gentlemen who are looking to pick up a woman and sometimes doles out some form of punishment to them. Also, if you try to take anything from her volcanoes or mountains, from her land, she will cause you bad luck and you have to return what you took to reverse that curse. So knowing this, while Tim and I were traveling up to Haleakala, one of the volcanoes on the Islands, as we're going up the mountain, I was getting a sense that she was there; there was a strong impression that I was feeling.

Timothy Green Beckley

Near the rim of the "House of the Sun" at Haleakala crater, Penny, Mayven and Tim seem to be up in the clouds as the Goddess Pele must surely be shining upon them in their travels this day.

And it was awe-inspiring. She left this tremendous feeling of peace and harmony with nature, and a strong sense that nature is something to be respected. Anyone who goes there can sense that as well, I'm sure. I felt tranquil and more connected to nature through her. Unfortunately, we didn't see her alongside the road, but that could be a good thing, because that showed maybe that we were welcome there, and that she accepted us as paying homage to her, as making a pilgrimage.

As the goddess of the volcano, she's the one that stole fire and brought it there, so she's in and of herself a fiery goddess. That is probably why women who are fire signs, such as myself, are very connected to it.

THE LINGERING BEAUTY OF THE KAHUNA

The strength of the Kahuna is just the essence of being connected to the people, to the land, and experiencing something that you can't find anywhere else. There's something special about the people there. There's something special about being there and allowing yourself to accept the energy that surrounds the Islands. It's fascinating, intoxicating, and they just overwhelm you with love and peace and acceptance.

I noticed that when we were there, on one side of the island, it was completely decimated by a volcano. It's almost like a borderline, where one part is the black lava ash. On the other side are these exotic flowers that would not be found anywhere on Earth except in this particular tropical climate. The beauty and the exotic nature of the land create this sense of wanting to know more about it, of wanting to be connected to it. I think that for people who don't live there on a daily basis, it has a strong mystique to it, and creates a desire to enter into this beauty, into the wildness of it. You're next to a volcano, and it could kill you, yet you're also standing next to this beauty and this rareness that can only be found there.

So I guess the magic that surrounds the Islands involves the idea that it has the two dynamics of ultimate destruction and power and force of fire, which is a very powerful element, and then you have the soft beauty and gentleness, the wonderful aura of the flowers and the flora of the Islands.

FIRST ENCOUNTER WITH THE DOLPHINS

Dolphins have been of great interest to me for many years, as they always seem to carry with them great wisdom. From a young age, I would dream about swimming with dolphins. They brought me a sense of security and peacefulness. Upon arriving in Hawaii, I found the urge to be with them overwhelming. The sleekness of their body and the unconditional love for humans attracted me to them in a subconscious way. I feel that I needed to know more about them and that to be close to them would help me to achieve that goal.

When I was asked by my close friend, Tim Beckley, to travel with him in exploration of these incredible animals, I quickly jumped to the ready. I was eager to be near them and experience their awe-inspiring love. I felt the days would not pass quickly enough. I wanted so much to be there with them already. I envied those that have had the incredible experience of swimming with them. I wanted my turn to be with them to be as magical and mystical as I hoped it would be.

While traveling out to sea with my daughter, Tim and Captain Nancy, I felt anxious. I was wondering if the dolphins would accept me into their ocean and be inspired to see me as I was to see them. I was not as experienced a skin diver as the others on the trip and I was also concerned for my daughter, who had never been on a boat. After an extensive talk about the dangers of not listening to the signals from the Captain and the way to properly approach them, I found that I was almost disillusioned about the trip when finally there was a sighting. A tremendous wave of calm and tranquility seemed to be sweeping towards us on the boat. I was again excited by the idea of being in the water with them.

Once the signal was given, we were told to enter the water. Our guide was an experienced surfer and diver who taught us the proper way to breathe through the snorkel. I became flustered and completely frightened that I would drown. I stayed above water and could not release the anxiety of using a snorkel. I would try to stay calm, but even though I was being guided through the steps, I would panic. Then, as if some greater force suddenly entered my mind, I was at peace. When I was fully able to comprehend what was happening, I realized I was among the dolphins. They were swimming around and under me, giving me help. I was able to swim along with them in their pod and my panic-induced breathing dissolved. I was freely swimming with them, and they watched as I tried to keep up. Once in a while one or two would play around me, observing my expressions and reactions as I calmly joined in their swim.

A DEEP AND PURIFYING LOVE

The second opportunity was just as amazing as the first, and I began to see the intoxicating effect they have on many swimmers. I wanted so much to dive down with them to their depths, but could not. So they came back to stay with me as I followed along. They were forgiving and open, loving and unsure, yet so powerful in their beauty. I was in awe of them and I thanked them for having me along for the ride. They put serene and positive images in my mind and they laughed as if they were happy to have met me. I knew in my heart that they would have immense love for us, and when I was near them, I could feel that love pouring into my soul. They made me feel pure and whole.

I miss that feeling. They brought with them a feeling of innocence and purity that I had not felt since I was a kid. I wanted so much to keep that feeling. I reminisce on the day that I spent out to sea with the dolphins, and my daughter and I talk often about our experience. She had a unique experience as well, and I love for her to talk about it. Although she was only three, she still talks about the friendly playful dolphins that surrounded her. She also had told me that they were protecting her. When I asked her to tell me more, she put it simply: "They told me that they loved us." And I believe they do.

After researching dolphins and their interactions, I felt that this experience happens often for many travelers to the sea. I read on many occasions that dolphins have been known to protect and save humans from a predator like a shark. The connection between our two species is far beyond our comprehension, and why it exists is even more puzzling to me. After all that has been done to them, from trapping in fishing nets to sport killing, they still have a drive to protect us and the curiosity to investigate us. I admire dolphins, and love them as closely as I would a fellow human. After all, they love us, do they not?

DOLPHINS AND THE ANCIENTS

Dolphins have mystified and evoked magical images for a long time. Why then is it now such a mystery to us that these magnificent creatures are so commonly held in high regard? Citizens of ancient Crete honored dolphins as gods, while the Greeks kept a special sanctuary for what they considered to be the dolphin god. Much art and jewelry is devoted to their image as well. Many stories and myths are based on events believed by people of the time to illustrate truthful and ethical ways of living.

One of the earliest dolphin stories is found in Homer's "Hymn To Apollo," which describes how the god Apollo founded the temple at Delphi after a long journey that took him all over Greece in search of a suitable site. Eventually he chose a lonely cave nestled at the foot of Mount Parnassus, which was guarded by the dragoness Python, whom he slew with an arrow from his silver bow. After killing the dragoness, Apollo set off to hijack a Cretan merchant ship, leaping aboard the boat in the guise of a dolphin. Terrified, the crew huddled below deck while the dolphin Apollo directed the winds to blow the ship right around the Greek coast and into the harbor below Delphi. Then, according to Homer's poem, the sun god instructed his hostages to live in the new temple and serve him as priests, saying: "And whereas I first, in the misty sea, sprung aboard the swift ship in the guise of a dolphin, therefore pray to me as Apollo Delphinus."

At the time Homer was writing this epic, there was a tremendous upheaval of religion and culture. The male-dominated sun god was beginning to replace the earlier earth mother image. But why a dolphin? One possibility is that the dolphin was introduced in one of the first political whitewash jobs in recorded history. By the time the story came to be written down, Delphi was already growing rich. The Delphic Oracle was a respected prophetess, and worshippers were traveling from all over Greece and beyond to consult her and to ask for Apollo's blessing. The petitioners had also taken to leaving handsome donations. Could it be that the name Delphi, with its allusion to the previous occupant, Delphos, the earth mother, was an embarrassment? "Delphos," the Greek for "dolphin," is a very similar word to "delplys," meaning "womb." If the association with the old religion was proving awkward, what better solution than to introduce a dolphin into the story and explain away the name by use of a clever pun?

So early cultures celebrated the divine features they saw in dolphins, renaming them because of the human love for them. Where has that gone in today's society? We may not see them as gods per se, but we are closely tied to them in feeling. We celebrate the unique tie we have and feel they are essentially "the humans of the sea."

CURRENT DOLPHIN RESEARCH

Today, research into life among wild dolphins reveals that they are curious and apparently sociable. Ancient Roman stories about boys riding on dolphins are likely true; in recent years, children as well as adults have ridden dolphins along the shores of the United States, Ireland, France, Spain, Yugoslavia, Australia and Great Britain. Dolphins have also been known to support drowning swimmers and nudge them to shore. So it is no wonder that they were viewed as gods by earlier cultures. The feelings I had when swimming with them could have been evoked through a primitive emotion that has not been explored as deeply in recent times. We may have forgotten, in essence, our real ties to these amazing mammals.

Dolphin research, which is just a few decades old, has caused much excitement. Some behavior studies have helped to verify certain ancient accounts. Although Aristotle recorded that fishermen in the eastern Mediterranean Sea could identify dolphins by the nicks in their fins, generations of humans, including scientists, dismissed it as fable. But Aristotle, who was the first to recognize that dolphins are air-breathing mammals and not fish, seems to have known what he was talking about. Why then are we surprised when a connection is made between our two species?

Because the rim of Haleakala volcano is located at the highest altitude to be found in North America, a "science city" has been set up containing an observatory and other semi-secret instillations. Definitely not open to "outsiders," all sorts of rumors have sprung up including various "dead aliens" being stored beneath one of the structures.

INNER LIGHT / GLOBAL COMMUNICATIONS
EXPLORING THE WORLD'S GREATEST MYSTERIES SINCE 1965

DISTRIBUTED BY GLOBAL COMMUNICATIONS

ORDER ALL TITLES FROM GLOBAL COMMUNICATIONS

Global Communications
Post Office Box 753
New Brunswick, New Jersey 08903

FOR OVER 40 YEARS Inner Light / Global Communications has brought to the world some of the best authors on Mysticism, Metaphysics, and the Unexplained. Our best recognized authors include: John A. Keel; Brad Steiger; Commander X; T. Lobsang Rampa; Tim Swartz; Timothy Green Beckley; William Alexander Oribello and Dragonstar.

OUR NUMBER ONE BEST SELLER!
OVER 50,000 COPIES IN PRINT!

THE LOST JOURNALS OF NIKOLA TESLA: HAARP—CHEMTRAILS AND THE SECRET OF ALTERNATIVE 4 by Tim Swartz

Discredited in his time, Nikola Tesla was made out by business competitors and the government to be nothing more than a crackpot. Nonetheless, these same conspirators later duplicated, and possibly even stole, many of Tesla's most famous inventions. Here is sensational data obtained from the inventor's most private papers and kept under wraps by military and big business concerns. Many of Tesla's most powerful and potentially dangerous scientific discoveries are being turned against ordinary citizens in programs of behavior and physical modification, including the seeding of clouds with mind and body altering chemicals. This book explores reverse gravity, free energy, contact with hidden dimensions, mysterious radio signals from space, earth changes, freak weather patterns, electric death rays, UFOs and particle beam weapons. ISBN: 1-892062-13-5 • $15.95

OTHER TESLA TITLES INCLUDE:
NIKOLA TESLA: FREE ENERGY AND THE WHITE DOVE by Commander X

Top Secret revelations by a former military intelligence operative regarding Tesla's secret propulsion system and how the Secret Government is flying anti-gravity craft. Reveals Tesla's "Cosmic Roots," and the existence of a remote underground site in Nevada where these craft are being hangared. ISBN: 0-938284-82-2 • $15.00

NIKOLA TESLA'S JOURNEY TO MARS—ARE WE ALREADY THERE? by Sean Casteel

Jules Verne wrote what was at the time considered to be far-fetched stories about the exploration of the moon and Mars. These classic literary works were based upon "wild rumors" circulating that such voyages had already occurred, with a group of scientists, all members of the same secret society. They had tapped into an unknown power source, using it to usher in the birth of flight years before the Wright Brothers flew their plane at Kittyhawk. Stranger than any fiction book could be, here is proof the NAZIs established colonies on the moon in the early 1940s; facts NASA doesn't want you to know! ISBN: 1-892062-31-3 • $14.95

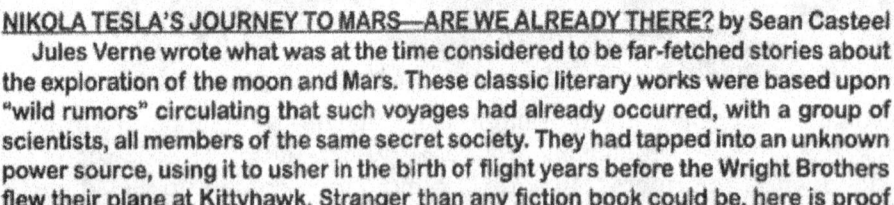

INVISIBILITY AND LEVITATION—HOW-TO KEYS TO PERSONAL PERFORMANCE by Commander X—Utilized by occultists and the martial arts, these are not parlor tricks, but actual methods adopted by the ancients and now used by the military intelligence community to perfect invisibility as demonstrated during the Philadelphia Experiment and Stealth Technology. This book offers various techniques that really work, providing the reader with dozens of examples which takes the subject out of its mystical surroundings. ISBN: 0-938294-36-9 • $15.95

CONTINUED ON NEXT PAGE >

SUBTERRANEAN WORLDS INSIDE EARTH by Timothy Green Beckley
Is the earth hollow? Is our planet honeycombed with caverns inhabited with a mysterious race? Are there civilizations of super beings living beneath the surface? Here are strange and unexplainable legends of the "Wee People," the Dero, and long-haired Atlantean giants! ISBN: 0-938294-22-1 • $14.95

THE DULCE WARS: UNDERGROUND ALIEN BASES AND THE BATTLE FOR PLANET EARTH by Branton
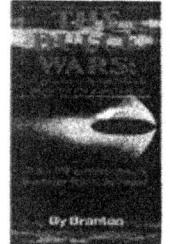
In the corner of a small town in America's Southwest, something very strange is going on! An alien Fifth Column is already active on Earth and may be preparing for global conquest. Dulce, New Mexico is the epicenter of cattle mutilations; energy grids; secret societies; underground anomalies; conspiracies between townfolk and "outsiders;" unexplained legends; lost civilizations, as well as abductions and missing time. ISBN: 1-892062-12-7 • $17.50

UFOS, PROPHECY AND THE END OF TIME by Sean Casteel
Is this mankind's final wakeup call? Explores Terrorism in America! Violence Overseas! War In The Middle East! Natural Disasters Worldwide! Man versus Nature! Religious Jihad, and unholy perversion in the Church. But, perhaps most important, almost ignored, is the worldwide appearance of UFOs and the abduction of humans by what may well be the "gods of old." This volume draws from Biblical prophecy and reliable UFOlogical sources and represents a divine revelation from The Heavenly Ones On High. ISBN 1-892062-35-6 • $16.95

THE LONG LOST BOOKS OF T. LOBSANG RAMPA FEATURING: MY VISIT TO AGHARTA by T. Lobsang Rampa—For decades Rampa's books brought great enlightenment, comfort and joy to millions who have repeatedly clambered for more of his enchanting narratives, despite the fact that he has been deceased for more than a decade. Recently a "lost" manuscript was discovered detailing Rampa's journey to Agharta, the sacred underground land in the hollow earth. This previously unknown land is populated by enlightened masters of great wisdom. Also in this book are excerpts from some of previously unavailable works. Topics include: Death and Life on the "Other Side;" Other Dimensions; Astral Projection; Contact With The Space Brothers. ISBN: 1-89206-34-5 • $19.95

MJ-12 AND THE RIDDLE OF HANGAR 18: THE NEW EVIDENCE by Timothy Green Beckley with Sean Casteel—Stored away in a secret underground hangar are the remains of the UFO that crashed at Roswell. According to the author, the last eight presidents have been in on the ultimate deception...a "Cosmic Watergate!" Over 60 cases of crashed UFOs are documented, offering proof of the existence of MJ-12 and the Interplanetary Phenomenon Unit involved in the recovery of crashed UFOs and their occupants. ISBN: 1-892062-53-4 • $24.95

NEW MAGICK HANDBOOK: SIMPLE SPELLS FOR A COMPLEX WORLD
by Dragonstar—Utilize everyday items to promote success: candles, crystals, herbs, gemstones, pendulum, charms, incantations and other proven methods of empowerment. The author is a mystic and occult adept who learned the science of alchemy and other universal laws. Here are spells and rituals to promote good health; encourage love; succeed in business; rid yourself of unwanted relationship and MORE!

ISBN: 1-892062-19-4 • $14.95

A NEW BOOK OF REVELATIONS as Channeled through Tuella—This work corrects many of the misconceptions and inaccurate translations of the Old and New Testaments and lays the foundation for a New Book of Revelations as transcribed from the highest spiritual powers of the Universe. Shocking revelations include: The true meaning of 666; The special significance of the 13th Vortex; How the Primary Channel for this work was able to thwart the forces of darkness and facilitate the departure of the "Fallen Ones;" How God's rebellious son Jehovahn inserted distortions into the original Biblical Scriptures to create disharmony; How a legion of Angels will protect you personally during a global war. Tuella's other works include: Project World Evacuation and Ashtar, A Tribute.
ISBN: 0-938-294-85-7 • $14.00

Global Communications, Box 753, New Brunswick, NJ 08903
Credit Card Orders 732 602-3407   MRUFO8@hotmail.com

FOR THOSE WISHING TO CONTACT MARIA CARTA
Those interested in a private consultation or a group reading -- or those who wish to address other business matters -- Maria Carta may be reached at marialeecarta61@gmail.com - Cell: 917 604-3912 Her Face Book Page Is: Maria Lee Carta Crescitelli, West Hills Ca. From time to time, Maria does readings and attends gatherings at the Malibu Coffee Bean - 310 598-7940

www.ingramcontent.com/pod-product-compliance
Lightning Source LLC
Chambersburg PA
CBHW080246170426
43192CB00014BA/2584